Preface

The book has been compiled by Pyarali Esmail Kassam. Pyarali Esmail Kassam was born East Africa in 1945. He was the son of Esmail Kassam from Mozambique, a merchant nicknamed as the "King without the Crown". Esmail Kassam grew up in wealth but moved to Mombasa after the collapse of his business. He moved to Old Port where he raised his children amid financial weakness.

Pyarali Kassam was the third child of Esmail Kassam and Sugrabai Kassam. He grew up in a conservative environment where education was restricted to the elite. He went to Alibhai Panju Primary school and then to Valentine High School. From there he went onto engineering studies at the Mombasa Institute.

In primary school, he met S.A Mehdi, the principal of Alibhai Panju school. S.A. Mehdi was fond of Pyarali and provided him with a number of life-long lessons which helped develop Pyarali's life. S.A. Mehdi himself a compiler wrote the book Parallelism of English and Urdu Poets. S.A. Mehdi always advised the author and told him about society, how to live a good life and be content and happy. Pyarali through his discussions with S.A. Mehdi became a fluent speaker of Lucknow urdu.

The author came from a modest upbringing where they had their struggles but he was contented with what they had and always believed in God to be the provider.

The author was a keen runner and learnt to swim at the age of 11. From then on he went to become Athletic and ~~swimming~~ champion. In 1963, he won the Uhuru Cup 2

1

In Mombasa, he became a swimming and diving champion. Jumping of from Fort Jesus. In one event during his youth, a boat had capsized, the author with his strong swimming skills volunteered and saved many peoples' lives.

He moved to Nairobi in 1973 where he acquired a job. Moving to Nairobi he invited his brother. In Nairobi he began his career in Kenya Ryan Mills (Textile Company). Then moved to Nine Ten investment where he learnt the PVC Trade of making Files, Bags and Blotters. From there he opened his own factory in 1977 and operated it until 2022.

The author enjoyed reading books especially on philosophy. The notable readers were Allama Iqbal (one of the greatest Muslim philosophers), Plato, Aristotle, Mir Anis and various others.

During his life, his viewpoints were considered very liberal in a conservative society. He believed in the development of the human race as he considered God has made the human the best of his creations where impossibility is just a state of mind.

During Covid while staying at home, he had an idea to compile all the famous sayings from all the people and bring it into a book. None of the quotes are from him but are from famous people. It should be noted that references have been made to all the famous people who have said the quotes. Where the individuals are unknown, these have been compiled in Section 3.

The aim of the book was to help readers in various stages of life to think about the issues, to learn from famous people and apply these to their own life. It is a book to help people better themselves. Many people question their existence, doubt their ambition and fear their goals. The individuals who made a change in the world knew their goal and wanted humanity to excel.

Pyarali Esmail Kassam playing football at a young age in Mombasa.

A collection of Trophies by Pyarali Esmail Kassam won during the National Uhuru Cup in 1963, Khunkar Walking Club

A young Pyarali Esmail Kassam reciting a poem in Momba

3

Contents Page

The book starts with the sayings of God as the master and creator.

Section 1 - Famous people and their quotations

 (in chronological order according to their era),

Section 2 - Quotations from different religions and proverbs

   from different countries,

Section 3 - Miscellaneous quotations by both famous and anonymous people

Section 4 - Life Stories and Lessons

99 DIRECT INSTRUCTIONS FROM ALLAH (GOD) TO MANKIND

1. Do not be rude in speech (3:15)

2. Restrain anger (3:134)

3. Be good to others (4:36)

4. Do not be arrogant (7:13)

5. Forgive others for their mistakes (7:199)

6. Speak to people mildly (20:44)

7. Lower your voice (31:19)

8. Do not ridicule others (49;11)

9. Be dutiful to your parents (17:23)

10. Do not say a word of disrespect to your parents (17:23)

11. Do not enter parents' private room without asking permission (24:58)

12. Write down the debt (2:282)

13. Do not follow anyone blindly (2:170)

14. Grant more time to repay if the debtor is in hard time (2:280)

15. Do not consume interest (2:275)

16. Do not engage in bribery (2:188)

17. Do not break promises (2:177)

18. Keep the trust (2:283)

19. Do not mix the truth with falsehood (2:42)

20. Judge with justice between people (4:58)

21. Stand out firmly for justice (4:135)

22. Wealth of the dead should be distributed among his family members (4:7)

23. Women also have the right for inheritance (4:7)

24. Do not devour the property of orphans (4:10)

25. Protect orphans (2:220)

26. Do not consume one another's wealth unjustly (4:29)

27. Try for settlement between people (9:49)

28. Avoid suspicion (12:49)

29. Do not spy and backbite (2:283)

30. Spend wealth in charity (57:7)

31. Encourage feeding the poor (107:3)

32. Help those in need by finding them (2:273)

33. Do not spend money extravagantly (17:24)

34. Do not invalidate charity with reminders (2:264)

35. Honor guests (15:26)

36. Order righteousness to people only after practicing yourself (2:44)

37. Do not prevent people from mosques (2:114)

38. Do not commit abuse on the earth (2:60)

39. Fight only with those who fight you (2:190)

40. Keep etiquette of war (2:191)

41. Do not turn back in battle (8:15)

42. No compulsion in religion (2:256)

43. Believe in all prophets (2:285)

44. Do not have sexual intercourse during menstrual period (2:222)

45. Breastfeed your children for the complete years (2:233)

46. Do not approach unlawful sexual intercourse (17:22)

47. Choose rules by their merit (2:247)

48. Do not burden a person beyond his scope (2:286)

49. Do not become divided (3:103)

50. Think deeply about the wonders and creation of this universe (3:191)

51. Man and woman have equal reward for their deeds (3:195)

52. Do not marry those in your blood relation (4:23)

53. Family should be led by men (4:34)

54. Do not be miserly (stingy) (4:37)

55. Do not keep envy (4:54)

56. Do not kill each other (4:92)

57. Do not be an advocate of deceit (4:105)

58. Do not cooperate in sin and aggression (5:2)

59. Cooperate in righteousness (5:2)

60. Having majority is not a criterion of truth (6:116)

61. Be just (5:8)

62. Punish for crimes in an exemplary way (5:38)

63. Strive against sinful and unlawful acts (5:63)

64. Dead animals, blood and the flesh of swine are prohibited (5:3)

65. Avoid intoxicants and alcohol (5:90)

66. Do not gamble (5:90)

67. Do not insult others' deities (6:108)

68. Do not reduce weight or measure to cheat people (6:152)

69. Eat and drink but be not excessive (7:31)

70. Wear good clothes during prayer times (7:31)

71. Protect and help those who seek protection (9:6)

72. Keep purity (9:108)

73. Never give up hope of Allah's mercy (12:87)

74. Allah will forgive those who have done wrong out of ignorance (16:119)

75. Invitation to God should be with wisdom and good instruction (16:125)

76. No one will bear other's sins (17:15)

77. Do not kill your children for fear of poverty (17:31)

78. Do not pursue that of which you have no knowledge (17:36)

79. Keep aloof from what is vain (23:3)

80. Do not enter others' houses without seeking permission (24:27)

81. Allah will provide security for those who believe only in Allah (24:55)

82. Walk on earth in humility (25:63)

83. Do not neglect your portion on this world (28:77)

84. Invoke not any other God along with Allah (28:88)

85. Do not engage in homosexuality (29:29)

86. Enjoin right forbid wrong (31:17)

87. Do not walk in silence through the earth (31:18)

88. Women should not display their finery (33:33)

89. Allah forgives all sins (39:53)

90. Do not despair of the mercy of Allah (39:53)

91. Repel evil by good (41:34)

92. Decide any affairs by consultation (42:38)

93. The most notable of you is the most righteous (49:13)

94. No monotheism in religion (57:27)

95. Those who have knowledge will be given higher degree by Allah (58:11)

96. Treat non-Muslims in a kind and fair manner (60:8)

97. Save yourself from covetousness (64:16)

98. Seek forgiveness of Allah, he is forgiving and merciful (73:20)

99. Do not consume one another's wealth unjustly (4:29)

Section 1

Quotations by names

HOMER

Greek poet (800 – 701 BC).

Quotations:

   i.   Give me a place to stand and I will move the earth.

   ii.   We men are wretched things.

   iii.   In youth and beauty, wisdom is but rare.

   iv.   A sound mind in a manly body.

   v.   For a friend with an understanding heart is worth no less than a brother.

   vi.   Sleep and death are twin brothers.

   vii.   The Lord gives and the Lord takes away, as it pleases him, for he can do all things.

   viii.   A small rock holds back a great wave.

   ix.   The difficulty is not so great to die for a friend; as to find a friend worth dying for.

   x.   Two friends, two bodies with one soul inspired.

   xi.   A sympathetic friend can be quite as dear as a brother.

LAO TZU

Chinese philosopher (6th century BC)

Quotations:

i.   Knowledge is treasure, but practice is the key to it.

ii. A man with outward courage dares to die; a man with inner courage dares to live.

iii. A journey of a thousand miles begins with a single step.

iv. If you would take, you must first give; this is the beginning of intelligence.

v.   If you want to become full, let yourself be empty.

vi. Mastering others is strength; mastering yourself is true power.

vii. He who knows that enough is enough will always have enough.

viii. If you correct your mind, the rest will fall into place.

ix. Greatest treasures: simplicity, patience, and compassion.

x.   Those who know do not talk; those who talk do not know.

xi. Be yourself without caring what others think.

xii. Change is inevitable, so embrace it, even if it seems uncomfortable.

xiii. Learn to follow first if you ever wish to lead.

xiv. Water is the softest thing, yet it can penetrate the mountain and the earth; this shows clearly the principle of softness overcoming hardness.

xv.   If you are depressed, you are looking in the past. If you are anxious you are living in the future. If you are at peace, you are living in the present.

xvi.   Always go with the flow.

xvii.   When you talk you are only repeating what you already know, but if you listen, you may learn something new.

xviii.   Silence is a source of great strength.

xix.   Respond intelligently even to unintelligent treatment.

xx.   Before healing others, heal yourself.

xxi.   Kindness in words creates confidence, kindness in thinking creates profoundness, kindness in giving creates love.

xxii.   Be still like a mountain and flow like a river.

xxiii.   He who is contented is rich.

xxiv.   He who controls others may be powerful; he who has mastered himself is mightier still.

xxv.   Knowing others is intelligence, knowing yourself is true wisdom; mastering others is strength, mastering yourself is true power.

xxvi.   To realize that you do not understand is a virtue; not to realize that you do not understand is a defect.

xxvii.   Knowing others is wisdom, knowing yourself is enlightenment.

xxviii.   Nature does not hurry, yet everything is accomplished.

xxix.   Doing nothing is better than being busy doing nothing.

GAUTHAMA BUDDHA

Religious leader (6th – 5th century BC)

Quotations:

i.   The greatest failure in life is stop trying.

   The greatest crime in life is disloyalty to partners.

   The greatest pity in life is self-depreciation.

   The greatest pride in life is revering for failure.

   The greatest wealth in life is health and wisdom.

   The greatest gift in life is acceptance.

   The greatest console is life is environment and charity.

ii.   To understand everything is to forgive everything.

iii.   The tongue like a sharp knife kills without drawing blood.

iv.   To conquer oneself is a greater task than conquering others.

v.   Better than a thousand hollow words is one word that brings peace.

vi.   Thousands of candles can be lit from a single candle, and the life of the candle will not be shortened.

vii.   Happiness never decreases by being shared.

viii.   If we could see the miracle of a single flower clearly, our whole life would change.

ix.   If we fail to look after others when they need help, who will look after us?

x.   Faith makes things possible, not easy.

xi. What you think you become, what you feel you attract, and what you imagine you create.

xii. Health is the greatest gift, contentment is the greatest wealth and faithfulness the best relationship.

xiii. Helping one person might not change the world, but it could change the world for one person.

xiv. You are the driver of your own life. Don't let anyone steal your seat.

xv. Even as a solid rock is unshaken by the wind so are the wise unshaken by the praise of blame.

xvi. Happiness comes when your work and words are benefit to others.

xvii. Three things cannot hide for long: the moon, the sun and the truth.

xviii. True love is born from understanding.

xix. If you truly loved yourself, you could never hurt another.

xx. However many holy words you read, however many you speak, what good will they do if you do not act on upon them?

xxi. An insincere friend is more to be feared then a wild beast.

xxii. Always be thankful for what you have, many people have nothing.

xxiii. Accept no one's definition of your life; define yourself.

xxiv. The distance between your dreams and reality is called action.

xxv.   Without patience nothing great can be achieved.

xxvi.   Happiness is not about getting what you want all the time. It is about loving what you have and being grateful for it.

xxvii.   Never judge people by their past.

People learn, people change, people move on.

xxviii. Buddhism is a philosophy of life; not a religion.

xxix.   When the Ego dies, the soul awakes.

xxx.   Mistakes are proof that you are trying.

xxxi.   It is okay to lose people but never lose yourself.

xxxii.   Without rain, nothing grows; learn to embrace the storms in your life.

xxxiii. Don't treat people as bad as they are, treat them as good as you are.

xxxiv.   If someone makes you happy, make them happier.

xxxv.   Stay soft, it looks beautiful on you.

xxxvi.   Words may lie but actions will always tell the truth.

xxxvii. Be patient, good things take time.

xxxviii. Be good to people for no reason.

xxxix.   Life is short, spend it with people who make you laugh and feel loved.

xl.   Be selective in your battles; sometimes peace is better than being right.

xli.   Silence isn't empty; it's full of answers.

xlii.   Don't let the behavior of others destroy your inner peace.

xliii. Helping a person will not necessarily change the world for that person.

xliv. Having somewhere to go is home, having someone to love is family, having both is a blessing.

xlv. Every morning we are born again. What matters is what we do today.

xlvi. Don't tell someone to get over it. Help them get through it.

xlvii. Your own salvation doesn't depend on others.

xlviii. You yourself must strive, the Buddha's only pointing the way.

xlix. Hate is not conquered by hate; hate is conquered by love. This is an eternal law.

l. If you have no actions to go with what you have learned, then you have learned nothing.

li. Rule your mind or it will rule you.

lii. Something good is coming today.

liii. If you light a lamp for someone else, it will also brighten your path.

liv. Negative thoughts will destroy you. Always keep a positive attitude.

lv. Don't ruin a good today by thinking about a bad yesterday. Let it go.

lvi. The moment you start acting like life is a blessing, it starts feeling like one.

lvii. You don't have a soul. You are a soul. You have a body.

lviii. The hardest battle is against yourself.

lix. Attachment leads to suffering.

lx. The mind is everything; what you think you become.

lxi. When you come to a point where you have no need to impress anybody, your freedom will begin.

lxii. A candle loses nothing by lighting another.

lxiii. Be where you are; otherwise you will miss your life.

lxiv. Patience is bitter but its fruit is sweet.

lxv. A meaningful silence is always better than meaningless words.

lxvi. One of the best lessons you can learn in life is to master how to remain calm.

lxvii. You only lose what you cling to.

lxviii. We were born to be real; not to be perfect.

lxix. People will throw stones at you. Don't throw them back. Collect them and build an empire.

lxx. I believe in the power of love.

lxxi. Train your mind to stay calm in every situation.

lxxii. Thank you God for always taking care of me.

lxxiii. Haters don't hate you. The reality is they fear they will never get to where you are now.

lxxiv. Yes, I am a nice person, but if you cross the line too many times, everything can change very quickly.

lxxv. It is not that I can't see what they see; it's that I see what they can't see.

lxxvi. If you want to be powerful educate yourself.

lxxvii. A moment of patience in a moment of anger saves you a hundred moments of regret.

lxxviii. There is no path to happiness; happiness is the path.

lxxix. You want to change your life? Change the way you think.

lxxx. Every day brings a choice: To practice stress or to practice peace.

lxxxi. True love is born from understanding.

lxxxii. Anything that costs you your peace is too expensive.

lxxxiii. You will not be punished for your anger. You will be punished by your anger.

lxxxiv. Be the same person privately, publicly and personally.

lxxxv. You will never change your life until you change something you do daily.

lxxxvi. The love of a family is life's greatest blessing.

lxxxvii. Apologize to children when you are wrong.

lxxxviii. Do not assume you are smarter than a child simply because you are older.

lxxxix. Say "thank you" to children when they do something for you or others.

xc. Admit when you have made a mistake and admit it openly to them.

xci. Listen to children.

xcii. Dead people receive more flowers than the living ones because regret is stronger than gratitude.

xciii.	Words may lie, but actions will always tell the truth.
xciv.	Never assume that the loud is strong and the quiet is weak.
xcv.	When writing the story of your life, don't let anyone else hold the pen.
xcvi.	When the wrong people leave your life, the right things start to happen.
xcvii.	Leave from everyone, follow no one.
xcviii.	A negative thinker sees a difficulty in every opportunity. A positive thinker sees an opportunity in every difficulty.
xcix.	The secret of a long life is laughter. The secret of a long lasting relationship is laughing together.
c.	I am a thinker; not a talker.
ci.	You need you more than you need them. Trust me.
cii.	Life is not a bad story; maybe you're just going through a bad chapter.
ciii.	The best revenge is no revenge; move on. Be happy.
civ.	If it doesn't challenge you, it won't change you.
cv.	Good people are like candles; they burn themselves up to give others light.
cvi.	One bad chapter doesn't mean your story is over.
cvii.	Remember somebody is happy with less than you have.
cviii.	Without patience, nothing great can be achieved.
cix.	Nobody can make you feel inferior without your consent.
cx.	Leaders don't force people to follow. They invite them on a journey.

cxi. Before you try to change others, just remember how hard it is to change yourself.

cxii. Never believe you are above or below anyone. Keep a humble spirit.

cxiii. Don't think too much. Just do what makes you happy.

cxiv. I trust the next chapter, because I am the author.

cxv. Life begins where fear ends.

cxvi. Never let your fear decide your future.

cxvii. Learn from yesterday, live for today, hope for tomorrow.

cxviii. No matter how educated, talented, rich or cool you are, how you treat people ultimately tells all; integrity is everything.

cxix. Without struggle, success has no value.

cxx. Do good for others; it will come back in unexpected ways.

cxxi. The hardest test in life is the patience to write for the right moment.

cxxii. Do not get upset with people or situations. Both are powerless without your reaction.

cxxiii. True love and loyal friends are the hardest things to find in life.

cxxiv. Stop expecting loyalty from people who can't even give you honesty.

cxxv. Nothing is permanent.

cxxvi.	Karma: Think good thoughts, say nice things, do good for others; everything comes back.
cxxvii.	Don't take revenge, let karma do all the work.
cxxviii.	Everybody is trying to find the right person, but nobody is trying to be the right person.
cxxix.	Be soft, do not let the world make you hard. Do not let pain make you hate. Do not let the bitterness steal your sweetness.
cxxx.	Don't believe in luck; believe in hard work.
cxxxi.	To be kind is more important than to be right. Many times what people need is not a brilliant mind that speaks but a special heart that listens.
cxxxii.	If you deeply observe everything, this is your teacher.
cxxxiii.	One moment can change a day, one day can change a life and one life can change the world.
cxxxiv.	Happy are those who take life day by day, complain very little and are thankful for the little things in life.
cxxxv.	Honesty saves everyone's time.
cxxxvi.	What we think we become.
cxxxvii.	Train your mind to see good in every situation.
cxxxviii.	Happy people focus on what they have. Unhappy focus on what is missing.
cxxxix.	Let the past make you better, not bitter.
cxl.	We are not given a good life or bad life. We are given a life. It is up to us to make it good or bad.

cxli.   Never stop learning because life never stops.

cxlii.   Six Rules of Life:

    a. Before you pray, believe.

    b. Before you speak, listen.

    c. Before you spend, earn.

    d. Before you write, think.

    e. Before you quit, try.

    f. Before you die, live.

cxliii.   Health is the greatest gift, contentment the greatest wealth, faithfulness is the best relationship.

cxliv.   If you want to be strong, learn to fight alone.

cxlv.   Don't judge others because you are not perfect.

cxlvi.   Kindness is the language which the deaf can hear and the blind can see.

cxlvii.   It takes three seconds to say "I love you"; three hours to explain why; and a lifetime to prove it.

cxlviii. Find out who you really are.

cxlix.   There are only two mistakes one can make along the road to the truth; not going all the way and not starting.

cl.   If you quit once, it becomes a habit.

cli.   Life is beautiful. One day, one hour and one minute will not come again in your entire life. Avoid fights, angriness and speak lovely to every person.

clii.   Expect nothing and appreciate everything.

cliii.	There are 4 very important words in life: love, truth, honesty and respect. Without these in your life, you have nothing.
cliv.	Attract what you want by being what you want.
clv.	Learn to take a break, not to quit.
clvi.	You cannot buy: i. Manners ii. Morals iii. Respect iv. Character v. Common sense vi. Trust vii. Patience viii. Class ix. Integrity x. Love
clvii.	Every day is a new beginning; take a deep breath and start again.
clviii.	Life is a one-time offer; use it well.
clix.	Trust the vibes you get, energy doesn't lie.
clx.	Happy people build their inner world. Unhappy people blame their outer world.
clxi.	A good laugh and a long sleep are the two best cures for anything.
clxii.	Better than a 1000 hollow words is one word that brings peace.
clxiii.	Ego never accepts the truth.
clxiv.	Money is the worst discovery of human life but it is the most trusted material to test human nature.

SOLON

Ancient Greek Philosopher

(630 – c. 560 BC)

Quotations:

i.   Learn to obey before you command.

ii.   Guide a friend in private and praise him in public.

iii.   I grow old learning something new every day.

iv.   In all things let reason be your guide.

v.   Rich people without wisdom and learning are but sheep with golden fleeces.

vi.   Speech is the mirror of action.

vii.   Put more trust in nobility of character than in an oath.

viii.   Laws are like spiders webs: if some poor weak creature comes up against them, it is caught, but a big one can break through and get away.

ix.   Seek to learn constantly while you live; do not wait in faith that old age will bring wisdom.

x.   As I grow older, I constantly learn more.

xi.   Angels are winged with God's power.

xii.   He who has learned how to obey will know how to command.

AESOP

Ancient Greek writer (620–564 BC)

Quotations:

   i.   No act of kindness, no matter how small it is, is ever wasted.

   ii.   Gratitude is the sign of noble souls.

   iii.   A liar will not be believed even when lie speaks the truth.

   iv.   It is not only fine feathers that make the fine birds.

   v.   We hang the petty thieves and appoint the great ones to public office.

   vi.   Appearances are often deceiving.

   vii.   Self-conceit may lead to self-destruction.

   viii.   Injuries may be forgiven but not forgotten.

   ix.   Do not count your chickens before they are hatched.

   x.   Please all and you will please none.

   xi.   Be content with your lot; one cannot be first in everything.

   xii.   Better be wise by the misfortune of others than by your own.

CONFUCIUS

Chinese philosopher and politician

(551- 479 BC)

Quotations:

i.   Respect yourself and others will respect you.

ii.   Forget injuries; never forget kindness.

iii.   I hear and I forget.

      I see and I remember.

      I do and I understand.

iv.   It does not matter how slowly you go so long to as you do not stop.

v.   By nature, men are nearly alike; by practice they get to be wide apart.

vi.   Wherever you go, go with all your heart.

vii.   There are some who bring a light so great to the world that even after they have gone the light remains.

viii.   The firm, the enduring, the simple and the modest are near to virtue.

ix.   Attack the evil that is within yourself, rather than attacking the evil that is in others.

x.   What the superior man seeks is in himself, what the mean man seeks is in others.

xi.   When you know a thing, to hold that you know it and when you do not know a thing, to allow that you do not know it, this is knowledge.

xii.   While you do not know life, how can you know about death?

xiii.   The man who says he can and the man who says he cannot….are both correct.

xiv.   Your life is what your thoughts make it.

xv.   The man who asks a question is a fool for a minute; the man who does not ask is a fool for life.

xvi.   The journey with 1000 miles begins with one step.

xvii.   Choose a job you love and you will never have to work a day in your life.

xviii.   You are what you think.

xix.   Silence is a friend who never betrays.

xx.   All people are the same; only their habits differ.

xxi.   We have two lives and the second begins when we realize we only have one.

xxii.   If you are the smartest person in the room, then you are in the wrong room.

xxiii.   Act with kindness but do not expect gratitude.

xxiv.   Worry not that no one knows you; seek to be worth knowing.

xxv.   The man who moves a mountain begins by carrying away a small stone.

xxvi.   The essence of knowledge is, having it to use it.

xxvii.   One joy dispels a hundred worries.

xxviii.	Anyone can find the switch after the lights are on.
xxix.	When you see a good person think of becoming like him/her.
xxx.	When you see someone not so good, reflect on your own weak points.
xxxi.	I slept and dreamt life is beauty; I woke and found life is duty.
xxxii.	He who knows all the answers has not been asked all the questions.
xxxiii.	Only the wisest and stupidest of men never change.
xxxiv.	Study the past if you would define the future.
xxxv.	If you make a mistake and do not correct it, this is called mistake.
xxxvi.	He who acts with a constant view to his own advantage will be much murmured against.
xxxvii.	If you look into your own heart and you find nothing wrong there, what is there to worry about? What is there to fear?
xxxviii.	When anger rises think of consequences.
xxxix.	The man of upright life is obeyed before he speaks.
xl.	Recompense injury with justice and recompense kindness with kindness.
xli.	Before you embark on a journey of revenge, dig two graves.
xlii.	He who will not economize, will have to agonize.

xliii.   Life is really simple but we insist on making it complicated.

xliv.   The gem cannot be polished without friction, nor man perfected without trials.

xlv.   You cannot open a book without learning something.

xlvi.   He who learns but does not think is lost; he who thinks but does not learn is in great danger.

SOCRATES

He was a classical Greek philosopher,
born in 469 BC and died in 399 BC.

Quotations:

i.   I am not Athenian or Greek but a citizen of the world.

ii.   Why do you care so much about laying up the greatest amount of money and honor and reputation, and so little about wisdom and truth and the greatest improvement of the soul?

iii. As for me all I know is that I know nothing.

iv.   An honest man is always a child.

v.   An unexamined life is not worth living.

vi.   He is richest who is content with the least, for content is wealth of nature.

vii. Education is the kindling of a flame; not the filling of a vessel.

viii. If all misfortune was laid in one heap hence everyone must take an equal portion, most people would be contented to take their own and depart.

ix.   If a man would move the world, he must first move himself.

x.   True wisdom comes to each of us when we realize how little we understand about life, ourselves, and the world around us.

xi.   Worthless people live only to eat and drink; people of worth eat and drink only to live.

xii.   Death may be the greatest of all human blessings.

xiii. The greatest way to live with honor in this world is to be what we pretend to be.

xiv.   He is a man of courage who does not run away but remains at his post and fights against the enemy.

xv.   Once made equal to man, woman becomes his superior.

xvi.   If a man is proud of his wealth, he should not be praised until it is known how he employs it.

xvii. He is not only idle who does nothing but he is idle who might be better employed.

xviii. Understanding a question is half an answer.

xix.   By all means marry; if you get a good wife, you will become happy; if you get a bad one you will become a philosopher.

xx.   May inward and outward man be one.

xxi.   Every action has its pleasure and its price.

xxii. Wisdom begins with wonder.

xxiii. It is not living that matters, but living rightly.

xxiv. There is only one good, knowledge, and one evil, ignorance.

xxv.   Strong minds discuss ideas, average minds discuss events, weak minds discuss people.

xxvi. It is better to suffer wrong than to do wrong.

xxvii. Mankind is made of two kinds of people; wise people who know they are fools, and fools who think they are wise.

xxviii.　Prefer knowledge to wealth for the one is transitory and the other perpetual.

xxix.　Sometimes you put up not to keep people out but to see who cares enough to break them down.

xxx.　The more I know the more I realize I know something.

xxxi.　To find yourself, think for yourself.

xxxii.　To know that you know nothing that is the meaning of knowledge.

xxxiii.　We can easily forgive a child who is afraid of the dark; the real tragedy of life is when men are afraid of the light.

xxxiv.　What screws us up the most in life is the picture in our head of what it is supposed to be.

xxxv.　Wonder is the beginning of wisdom.

xxxvi.　I cannot teach anybody anything; I can only make them think.

xxxvii.　We cannot live better than by seeking to become better.

xxxviii.　I know that I am intelligent because I know that I know nothing.

xxxix.　Be slow to fall into friendship but when you are in, continue firm and constant.

HIPPOCRATES

Greek physician of the Classical period
(460 – 370 BC)

Quotations:

i.   Let food be your medicine and medicine be your food.

ii.   Wherever the art of medicine is loved, there is also a love of humanity.

iii.   Walking is man's best medicine.

iv.   Natural forces within us are the true healers of disease.

v.   If we could give every individual the right amounts of nourishment and exercise, not too little and not too much, we would have found the safest way to health.

vi.   A wise man should consider that health is the greatest of human blessings and learn how by his own thought to derive benefit from his illness.

vii.   It is more important to know what sort of person has a disease than to know what sort of disease a person has.

viii.   Sport is a preserver of health.

ix.   The physician treats, but nature heals.

PLATO

Greek philosopher
(428 BC - 348 BC).

Quotations:

i. Wise men speak because they have something to say, fools because they have to say something.

ii. At the touch of lover everyone become a poet.

iii. Do not train a child to learn by force or harshness; but direct them to it by what amuses their minds, so that you may be better able to discover with accuracy the peculiar bent of the genius of each.

iv. The measure of a man is what he does with power.

v. Courage is to know what not to fear.

vi. Better a little which is well done than a great…imperfectly.

vii. One of the penalties for refusing to participate in politics is that you end up being governed by your inferiors.

viii. Man can discover more about a person in an hour of play than in a year of conversation.

ix. For the man to conquer himself is the first and noblest of all victories.

x. The greatest wealth is to live content with little.

xi. A good decision is based on knowledge; not numbers.

xii.   The heaviest penalty for declining to rule is to be ruled by someone inferior.

xiii.   There are three classes of men; lovers of wisdom, lovers of honor and lovers of gain.

xiv.   In politics we presume that everyone who knows how to get votes knows how to administer a city or a state. When we are ill, we do not ask for the handsomest physician or the most eloquent one.

xv.   You should not honour men more than truth.

xvi.   The object of education is to teach us to love what is behaviour.

xvii.   A house that has liberty in it has a soul.

xviii. When there is an income tax the just man will pay more and the unjust less on the same amount of income.

xix.   Knowledge is the food of the soul.

xx.   The great words never die.

xxi.   The beginning is the most important part of the work.

xxii.   The greatest wealth is to live content with little.

xxiii. For a man to conquer himself is the first and noblest of all victories.

xxiv.   All the gold, which is under or upon the earth, is not enough to give in exchange for virtue.

xxv.   Ideas are the sources of all things.

xxvi.   Human behavior flows from three main sources; desire, emotion and knowledge.

ARISTOTLE

He was an ancient Greek philosopher who was born in 384 BC and died in 322 BC. His writings cover many subjects and comprise the first comprehensive system of western philosophy.

Quotations:

i. Education is an ornament in property and refuge in adversity.

ii. Educating the mind without educating the heart is no education at all.

iii. We are what we repeatedly do.

iv. Wicked men obey from fear and good men from love.

v. What is a friend? A single soul dwelling in two bodies.

vi. Men cling to life even at the cost of enduring great misfortune.

vii. Teaching is the highest form of understanding.

viii. All men by nature desire knowledge.

ix. The educated differ from the uneducated as much as the living differ from the dead.

x. Happiness depends upon ourselves.

xi. Knowing yourself is the beginning of all wisdom.

xii. He who has overcome his fear will truly be free.

xiii.   Hope is a walking dream.

xiv.   Quality is not an act; it is a habit.

xv.   Fear is a pain arising from anticipation of evil.

xvi.   We make war that we may live in peace.

xvii.   Nature does nothing in vain.

xviii.   The greatest virtues are those which are most useful to other persons.

xix.   The worst form of inequality is to try to make unequal things equal.

xx.   Good habits formed at youth make all the difference.

xxi.   To avoid criticism do nothing, say nothing and be nothing.

xxii.   The more you know, the more you know you don't know.

CHANAKYA

Ancient Indian polymath (375–283 BC)

Quotations:

i. A man is great by deeds; not by birth.

ii. As soon as fear approaches, attack and destroy it.

iii. The poor wish for wealth; animals for the faculty of speech; men wish for heaven; Godly persons for liberation.

iv. Those base men who speak of the secret faults of others destroy themselves like serpents that stray onto anthills.

v. The biggest Guru mantra is never sharing your secrets with anybody; it will destroy you.

vi. Once you start working on something don't be afraid of failure and don't abandon it; people who work sincerely are the happiest.

vii. As a calf follows its mother among a thousand cows so the (good or bad) deeds of a man follow him.

ALEXANDER THE GREAT

King of the ancient Greek kingdom of Macedonia (356 – 323 BC)

Quotations:

i. I am not afraid of an army of lions led by a sheep; I am afraid of an army of sheep led by a lion.

ii. There is nothing impossible to him who will try.

iii. I am indebted to my father for living but to my teacher for living well.

iv. I had rather excel others in knowledge of what is excellent than in the extent of my power and dominion.

v. I would rather live a short life of glory than a long life of obscurity.

vi. God must have loved Afghans because he made them so beautiful.

vii. But truly, if I were not Alexander I would be Diogenes.

viii. Bury my body and don't build a monument, keep my hands out so the people know the one who won the world had nothing in hand when he died.

ix. In the end, when it's over, all that matters is what you have done.

EPICURUS

Ancient Greek Philosopher (341–270 BC)

Quotations:

  i.   The art of living well and the art of dying well are one.

  ii.   It is folly for a man to pray to the Gods for that which he has the power to obtain by himself.

 iii.   The misfortune of the wise is better than the prosperity of the fool.

 iv.   Nothing is enough for the man to whom enough is too little.

  v.   If God listened to the prayers of men, all men would have quickly perished; for they are forever praying for evil against one another.

ZENO OF CITIUM

Greek philosopher (334 – 262 BC)

Quotations:

i.   By silence, I hear other men's imperfections.

ii. The avaricious man is like the barren, sandy ground of the desert, which sucks in all the rain and dews with greediness but yields no fruitful herbs or plants for the benefit of others.

iii. Better to trip with the feet than with the tongue.

iv. No evil is honourable but death is honourable; therefore death is not evil.

v.   All the good are friends of one another.

MARCUS TULLIUS CICERO

Roman politician (106 – 43 BC)

Quotations:

i. A happy life consists in traditionality of mind.

ii. While there's life there's hope.

iii. To err is human, but to persevere in error is only the act of a fool.

iv. Life is nothing without friendship.

v. Life without learning is death.

vi. Probability is the very guide of life.

vii. I am not ashamed to confess I am ignorant of what I do not know.

viii. Our span of life is brief, but is long enough for us to live well and honestly.

ix. The function of wisdom is to discriminate between good and evil.

x. Sometimes I do what I want to do, the rest of the time I do what I have to.

xi. What then is freedom? The power to live as one wishes.

xii. To live long, live slowly.

xiii. Nobody can give you wiser advice than yourself.

xiv. An unjust peace is better than a just war.

xv.   Next to God we are nothing, to God we are everything.

VIRGIL

Roman Poet (70 – 19 BC)

Quotations:

i.   Start with the most important.

ii.   They can do all because they can.

iii.   Fortune favors the brave.

iv.   Death is the brother of sleep.

v.   Let us go singing as far as we go; road will be less tedious.

vi.   Love conquers all things; let us too surrender to love.

HORACE

Roman poet (65 – 8 BC)

Quotations:

   i.   A picture is a poem without words.

   ii.   Anger is a short madness.

   iii.   Life is largely a matter of expectation.

   iv.   Don't think, just do.

   v.   Whatever advice you give, be short.

   vi.   I teach that all men are mad.

   vii.   Leave rest to the God.

   viii.   Imitators, you slavish herd.

   ix.   The pen is the tongue of the mind.

   x.   A word, once sent abroad, flies irrevocably.

   xi.   Begin, be bold and venture to be wise.

   xii.   In adversity remember to keep an even mind.

   xiii.   Adversity reveals genius, prosperity conceals it.

   xiv.   Undeservedly you will atone for the sins of your fathers.

   xv.   Subdue your passion or it will subdue you.

SENECA

Roman philosopher and advisor of

The Roman emperor Nero (4 BC- 65 AD)

Quotations:

i. All cruelty springs from weakness.

ii. Sometimes even to live is an art of courage.

iii. Life if well lived is long enough.

iv. As long as you live, keep learning how to live.

v. Wealth is the slave of the wise, the master of the fool.

vi. It is not the man who has too little but the man who craves more who is poor.

vii. He who is brave is free.

viii. He is the most powerful who has power over himself.

ix. No man was ever wise by chance.

x. Time heals what reason cannot.

xi. If you wish to be loved, love.

xii. Throw me to the wolves and I will return leading the pack.

xiii. While we teach, we learn.

xiv. It is not that we have a short time to live but that we waste a lot of it.

xv. Difficulties strengthen the mind as labour does the body.

xvi. Life is long if you know how to live it.

xvii. It is of course better to know useless things than to know nothing.

xviii. No nation can rise to the height of glory unless your women are side by side with you.

xix. My message to you all is of hope, courage and confidence.

xx. That man lives badly who does not know how to die well.

xxi. The wise man will live as long as he ought not as long as he can.

EPICTETUS

Greek Stoic Philosopher (50 – 138 AD)

Quotations:

 i. Books are the training weights of mind.

 ii. Never say you are alone for you are not alone, your God and your genius are within.

 iii. Only the educated are free.

 iv. It is not what happens to you, but how you react to it that matters.

 v. We have two ears and one mouth so that we can listen twice as much as we can speak.

 vi. Wealth consists not in having great possessions but in having few wants.

 vii. Men are disturbed not by having things but by the view which they take of them.

 viii. First say to yourself what you would be and then do what you have to.

 ix. If you want to improve, be content to be thought foolish and stupid.

 x. No man is free who is not a master of himself.

 xi. He is a wise man who does not grieve for the things which he has not but rejoices for those which he has.

xii. Man is not worried by real problems so much as by his imagined anxieties about real problems.

xiii. He who laughs at himself never runs out of things to laugh at.

xiv. Freedom is the only worthy goal in life. It is won by disregarding things that lie beyond our control.

xv. Circumstances don't make the man; they only reveal him to himself.

xvi. It's impossible for a man to learn what he thinks he already knows.

xvii. You are a little soul caring around a corpse.

xviii. First learn the meaning of what you say and then speak.

xix. Seek not the good in external things, seek it in yourselves.

xx. Do not try to seem wise to others.

xxi. A ship should not ride on a single anchor nor life on a single hope.

xxii. Know first who you are and then adorn yourself accordingly.

xxiii. If you would be a reader, read. If a writer, write.

xxiv. Someone asked, who is a rich man? Epictetus replied, he who is content.

xxv. It is better to die of hunger having lived without grief and fear, than to live with a troubled spirit amid abundance.

xxvi. Small minded people blame others, average people blame themselves, the wise see all blame as foolishness.

xxvii.	Give me by all means a shorter and nobler life instead of one that is longer but of less account.
xxviii.	No great thing is created suddenly.
xxix.	You may fetter my leg but Zeus himself cannot get the better of my free will.
xxx.	What concerns me is not the way things are, but the way people think things are.
xxxi.	Don't live by your own rules, but in harmony with nature.
xxxii.	Do not explain your philosophy, embody it.
xxxiii.	The key is to keep company only with people who uplift you; whose presence calls forth your best.

MARCUS AURELIUS

Roman emperor (121- 180 AD)

Quotations:

i.   If it's not right, don't do it. If it's not true, don't say it.

ii.   The best revenge is not to be like your enemy.

iii.   Accept the things to which fate binds you and love the people with whom fate brings you together but do so with all your heart.

iv.   Confine yourself to the present.

v.   Straight; not straightened.

vi.   When you arise in the morning, think of what a precious privilege it is to be alive – to breathe, to think, to enjoy, to love.

vii.   Whatever happens to you has been waiting to happen since the beginning of time.

viii.   That which is not good for the bee-hive cannot be good for the bees.

ix.   To live happily is an inward power of the soul.

x.   You can commit injustice by doing nothing.

xi.   Waste no more time arguing about what a good man is; be one.

xii.   Do every act of your life as if it were your last.

xiii.   It is not death that a man should fear but he should fear never beginning to live.

xiv.   Each day provides its own gifts.

xv. Anger cannot be dishonest.

xvi. Nothing should be done without a purpose.

xvii. Even the smallest thing should be done with reference to the end.

xviii. Stick to what is in front of you – idea, action, utterance.

xix. What is your art? To be good.

xx. Kindness is unconquerable.

xxi. Give yourself a gift: The present moment.

xxii. What illusion about myself do I entertain?

xxiii. A rational animal is consequently also a social animal.

xxiv. Glory is an empty changeable thing, as fickle as the weather.

xxv. Poverty is the mother of crime.

xxvi. A man should be upright; not be kept upright.

xxvii. Our life is what our thoughts make it.

xxviii. The only wealth which you will keep forever is the wealth you have given away.

xxix. Because anything seems difficult for you, do not think it is impossible for anyone to accomplish.

xxx. It never ceases to amaze me: we all love ourselves more than any other people but care more about their opinions than our own.

xxxi. When you live while it is still in your power be a decent man.

PROPHET MUHAMMAD S.A.W.

Last Prophet in Islam. Arab political leader (570 – 632 AD)

Quotations:

i.   Say I believe in Allah (God), then adhere firmly to that.

ii.   He is not one of us who does not have mercy on your young and does not respect our elders.

iii.   The most humiliating person is the one who insults others.

iv.   The best way to protect Islam is to practice Islam.

v.   He who eats to his fill while the neighbour goes without food, is not a believer.

vi.   There are no two Muslims who meet and shake hands with one another, but they will be forgiven before they part.

vii.   The pardon of God is greater than your sins.

viii.   Speak well or remain silent.

ix.   Beware of lying for lying leads to wickedness and wickedness leads to the hell.

x.   A smart person knows what to say.
A wise person knows whether or not to say it.

xi.   Do not withhold your money (otherwise) God would withhold his blessings from you.

xii.   The best of all charities is to deal a hungry person.

xiii.   Be large of heart and success, be small of heart and fail.

xiv. The most hated person in the eyesight of God is the most quarrelsome.

xv. God is in front of you when you pray.

xvi. Silence is an ocean. Speech is a river. When the ocean is searching for you, don't walk in the river; hear the ocean.

xvii. The strong is not the one who overcomes the people by his strength, but the strong is the one who controls himself while in anger.

xviii. The best of you is he who learn the Quran and teaches it.

xix. Most of your sins are because of your tongues.

xx. Act kindly towards women.

xxi. Kindness is a mark of faith, and whoever is not kind has no faith.

xxii. The strongest among you is the one who controls his anger.

xxiii. Islam has raised the status of woman from below the earth to so high that paradise lies at her feet.

xxiv. Be in this world like a stranger or one who is passing through.

xxv. Whoever loves to meet God, God loves to meet him.

xxvi. I and the one who looks after an orphan, will be together like this in the next world.

xxvii. Richness is not having many possessions, but richness is being content with oneself.

xxviii. If you show mercy to those who are on the earth, he who is in the heaven will show mercy to you.

xxix.	You do not do evil to those who do evil to you, but you deal with them with forgiveness and kindness.
xxx.	Even a smile is charity.
xxxi.	Verily God does not look to your faces and your wealth but he looks to your heart and your deeds.
xxxii.	There is a reward for kindness to every living thing.
xxxiii.	A white has no superiority on a black nor a black has any superiority over a white except by piety and good action.
xxxiv.	A father gives his child nothing better than a good education.
xxxv.	The best of you are those who are best to the women.
xxxvi.	The cure for ignorance is to question.
xxxvii.	If a man parses you too much throw dust on his face.
xxxviii.	I love children. They are content with the least of things; gold and mud are the same in their eyes.
xxxix.	The best among you is the one who doesn't harm others with his tongue and hands.
xl.	Exchange gifts, you will love one another.

IMAM ALI (A.S)

1st Divinely appointed Imam. Son-in-law and companion of the Islamic prophet Muhammad (600 – 661 AD)

Quotations:

i. Verily if you become humble, God will elevate you.

ii. Maintaining silence with the fool is the best response.

iii. Hate is inherited the same way wealth is inherited.

iv. There are two reasons, why we don't trust people; first, we don't know them; second, we know them.

v. Even if you are a leader you are just a servant of God.

vi. Sit with the poor and your gratefulness will increase.

vii. Courtesy costs nothing but buys everything.

viii. Take lessons from history for your future, because history often repeats itself.

ix. Your friends are many when you count them, but in hardships they become few.

x. Aid your brother in every situation and go with him wherever he goes.

xi. Whoever guides someone to goodness will have a similar reward.

xii. Help and you will be helped.

xiii. The world cannot defeat you unless you accept defeat.

xiv. Whoever is good to his parents, his child will be good to him.

xv. Beware of apprehension, for it kills hope, weakens actions and brings about worry.

xvi. Pray for others before praying for yourself.

xvii. Half of your beauty comes from the way you speak.

xviii. Do not be ashamed of saying "I don't know."

xix. The winds do not blow to make trees dance but to test their roots.

xx. Who speaks to you about others, will speak about you to others.

xxi. One who informs you of your faults is indeed your friend.

xxii. Better than a beautiful face is a beautiful heart and better than a beautiful word is a beautiful deed.

xxiii. Brothers are the best of assets in the times off hardship.

xxiv. One who pretends to be poor, becomes poor.

xxv. A hypocrite's words are beautiful, but his actions are painful malady.

xxvi. It is easier to turn a mountain into dust than to create love in a heart that is filled with hatred.

xxvii. The cheater has a sweet tongue and a bitter heart.

xxviii. Truth is heavy and difficult but pleasant and falsehood is light and easy but painful and dangerous.

xxix. The best revenge is to improve yourself.

xxx. People often hate those things which they do not know or cannot understand.

xxxi. Speak only when your words are more beautiful than silence.

xxxii. Do not feel ashamed if the amount of charity you give is small, because to refuse the needy is an act of greater shame.

xxxiii. Hide the good you do and make known the good done to you.

xxxiv. When words come from the heart of anyone they find a place in the heart of another.

xxxv. Never make a decision in anger and never make a promise in happiness.

xxxvi. A bad deed which you regret in your heart is a thousand times better than the good deed that makes you proud.

xxxvii. Don't use the shortness of your speech on the mother who taught you to speak.

xxxviii. If you want to know where your heart is, see where your mind goes when it wonders.

xxxix. If you want to eliminate evil from the heart of others, then first uproot it from your own.

xl. Strength doesn't lie in carrying heavy loads, camels can do that. Strength lies in controlling your temper.

xli. The days of life pass away like clouds, so do good while you are alive.

xlii. Keep praying for what it is you seek; impossibility and possibility are merely concepts of your mind. To Allah (God), nothing is impossible.

xliii. Generosity is to help a deserving person without his respect and if you need help him after his request, then it is either out of self-respect or to avoid rebuke.

xliv. Surely silence can sometimes be the most eloquent reply.

xlv. Our enemies are not Jews or Christians but our enemy is our own ignorance.

xlvi. How foolish is man. He ruins the present while worrying about future but weeps in the future by recalling his past.

xlvii. A liar's biggest punishment in this world is that even his truth is rejected.

xlviii. A friend cannot be considered a friend until he is tested in three occasions;

- In time of need
- behind your back
- after your death.

xlix. If you like to see your prayers answered during hard times, you must pray hard during easy times.

l. How strange is man that when he is afraid of something he runs away from it but when he is afraid of Allah he gets closer to him.

li. There are six situations in which the intellects of people are tested:

1. Association, 2. Transaction, 3. Authority, 4. Isolation, 5. Affluence, 6. Poverty.

lii.   A true friend is one who upon seeing a fault gives you advice and defends you in your absence.

liii.   There is no garment more beautiful than vitality.

liv.   If you want to identify someone's character, examine the friends he sits with.

lv.   Knowledge is better than wealth. Knowledge guards you while you have to guard wealth.

lvi.   Knowledge is a ruler while wealth is ruled upon.

lvii.   You find that the human beings' tongue is light, yet its power is so devastating.

lviii. For your brother offer blood and wealth, for your enemy your justice and fairness and for people in general, your joy and good favor.

lix.   Never explain yourself to anyone because the one who likes you would not need it and the one who dislikes you would not believe it.

lx.   See the bad inside yourself and see the good inside others.

lxi.   Aim to live in this world without allowing the world to live inside you because when a boat sits on water it sails perfectly but when water enters inside the boat it sinks.

lxii.   Do not show pleasure in somebody's downfall, for you have no knowledge of what the future holds in store for you.

lxiii. A man of wealth has many enemies while a man of knowledge has many friends.

lxiv.	He who indulges in jokes and loose talk loses a part of his wisdom.
lxv.	I am astonished at those people who, when you respect them, they disrespect you and if you disrespect them they respect you.
lxvi.	A moment of patience in a moment of anger saves a thousand moments of regret.
lxvii.	Patience is that a man bears whatever afflicts him and swallows his anger.
lxviii.	Be an enemy to the oppressor and a helper to the oppressed.
lxix.	Do not close a door that you are unable to open.
lxx.	Bear sorrows and calamities patiently; otherwise, you will never be happy.
lxxi.	A saga sees things through his insight; a fool through his illusive vision.
lxxii.	Every breath of man brings him closer to death.
lxxiii.	If you commit misdeed, hasten to erase it with repentance.
lxxiv.	The value of each man depends upon the art and skills he has attained.
lxxv.	No shelter is safer than piety.
lxxvi.	Eat pears for they polish the heart.
lxxvii.	Increase your silence and your thoughts will flourish, your heart will enlighten and people will be safe from your hands.
lxxviii.	The wiser the man the less talkative will he be.

lxxix.	Whoever commits a sin without intention is worth of forgiveness.
lxxx.	One who adopts patience will never be deprived of success though it may take a long time to teach him.
lxxxi.	My mother named me Haider, I attack like the lion of the jungle and no one can escape from my attack.
lxxxii.	The most complete gift of God is a life based on knowledge.
lxxxiii.	Do not run after the one who tries to avoid you.
lxxxiv.	Do not make promises unless you can keep it.
lxxxv.	Do not be sorry about anything in this world that you have been denied.
lxxxvi.	God has placed ease and comfort in paradise but people look for it in this world and do not find it.
lxxxvii.	People are asleep as long as they are alive; when they die, they wake up.
lxxxviii.	The knowledge which remains only on your tongue is very superficial. The intrinsic value of knowledge is that you act upon it.
lxxxix.	A fool mind is at the mercy of his tongue and wise man's tongue is under the control of his mind.
xc.	A wise man first thinks and then speaks and a fool speaks first and then thinks.
xci.	Not to have a thing is less humiliating than to beg it.

xcii. Patience is of two kinds; patience over what pains and patience against what you covet.

xciii. Anything which can be counted is finite and will come to an end.

xciv. Live amongst people in such a manner that if you die they weep over you and if you are alive they crave for your company.

xcv. The best deed of a great man is to forgive and forget.

xcvi. If you cannot get things as much as you desire then be contended with what you have.

xcvii. An ignorant person will always overdue a thing or neglect it totally.

xcviii. I wonder at a man who loses hope of salvation when the door of repentance is open for him.

xcix. When someone is sure of returns then he shows generosity.

c. One who guards his secrets has complete control over his affairs.

IMAM HUSSEIN (A.S)

Third divinely appointed Imam

(626 – 680 AD)

Quotations:

i.   To me, death is nothing but happiness and living under tyrants nothing but living in Hell.

ii.   Hastiness is foolishness.

iii.   One who reveals your faults to you like a mirror is your true friend, and one who flatters you and covers up your faults is your enemy.

iv.   Best of wealth is that which one protects his fame and dignity.

v.   He who has you (God) has everything and he who has deprived himself of you is the poorest in the world.

vi.   If you do not believe in any religions and don't fear the resurrection day, at least be free in this world.

vii.   The needy one loses his respect by asking you. So do not lose your respect by denying him.

viii.   Telling the truth brings about honour.

ix.   Among the signs of ignorance is arguing with irrational people.

x.   Wisdom will not be complete by following the truth.

xi.   The most merciful person is the one who forgives when he is able to take revenge.

IMAM JAFAR AL SADIQ

6th Divinely appointed Imam

(702 – 765AD)

Quotations:

   i.   Justice is sweeter than the water of the thirsty person.

   ii.   How wide justice is even if very little.

   iii.   If you want to know the religion of a man, do not look at how much he prays and fasts; rather look at how he treats people.

   iv.   The best man is he who in whom four traits have come together:

     a.   If he does well, he is cheerful.

     b.   If he does badly, he asks for forgiveness.

     c.   If he is wrong, he forgives.

     d.   If he is afflicted, he is patient.

   v.   Anger is the destruction of a wise man.

   vi.   Whoever doesn't control his anger doesn't control his intellect.

   vii.   Whoever is satisfied with what Allah (God) has given him then he is the richest of men.

   viii.   The most perfect of men in intellect is the best of them in ethics.

   ix.   Nothing is better than silence.

x. The perfection of intellect is in three things; humbleness for Allah (God), good certainty and silence except for good.

xi. No illness is more dangerous than telling lies.

xii. If a person gains knowledge and does not act upon it, it is just like a person who has treasure and does not use it.

xiii. Verily, the parallel of the life in this world is like the parallel of the water of the sea.

xiv. Whatever the thirsty drink of it, they increase in thirst until it kills them.

xv. Indeed the parallel of the life in this world is like the parallel of the snake whose touching is smooth whilst the lethal poison is inside it, the wise man is careful of it.

xvi. Indeed the parallel of life in this world is like the parallel of the silkworm. The more it wraps itself with silk, the more it will be difficult for it to go out till it dies of worry.

xvii. Seek knowledge and adorn it with forbearance and dignity, be humble to whom you teach and to those whom you learn. Don't be tyrannical in your teaching conduct, for you will forfeit that
to which you are entitled to the reward on account of it.

xviii. The person who is aware of the present situations of his time, will never be involved with falsifying and wrongdoing.

xix. A learned person among ignorant people is like a person among the dead.

xx. Write knowledge since you can't memorize unless with writing. Heart confides to the written.

xxi. There are two kinds of scholars; those who act on their knowledge; these are the saved ones; and those who do not put into practice what they know, these are led to their downfall.

ALI GHAZALI

Persian Islamic philosopher who was born in 1058 and died in 1111.

Quotations:

    i.   A man of bad character punishes his own soul.

    ii.   Those who look for seashells will find seashells.
        Those who open them will find pearls.

    iii.   Real friend is the one who, when you ask him to follow you, doesn't ask where? But gets up and goes.

    iv.   What is destined will reach you, even if it is beneath two mountains. What is not destined will not reach you, even if it be between your two lips.

    v.   Tongue is very small and light but can take you to the greatest heights and it can put you in the lowest depths.

    vi.   The hypocrite looks for faults; the believer looks for excuses.

    vii.   Desire makes slaves of kings, patience makes kings out of slaves.

    viii.   Soft words soften the hearts that are harder than rock. Harsh words harden hearts that are softer than silk.

    ix.   Advice is easy, what is difficult is accepting it for it is better in taste.

x. If you see a scholar speaking ill of other scholars, avoid him.

xi. Take every effort to guard your tongue as it is the strongest cause of your destruction in this life and the next.

xii. The first stage of sincerity is that your private and public state is the same.

xiii. Declare war on 12 enemies you cannot see:

1. Egoism. 2. Arrogance 3. Conceit. 4. Selfishness 5. Greed 6. Lust 7. Intolerance 8. Anger 9. Lying 10. Cheating 11. Gossiping 12. Slander.

GENGHIS KHAN

The first Emperor of the Mongol

Empire (1162 - 1227)

Quotations:

i.   If you are afraid don't do it. If you are doing it don't be afraid.

ii.   I am the flail of God; had you not created great sins God would not have sent a punishment like me upon you.

iii.   Even when a friend does something you don't like, he continues to be your friend.

iv.   There is no God in anything until it is finished.

v.   Concurring the world on horseback is easy. It is the dismounting and the governing that is hard.

vi.   A leader can never be happy until his people are happy.

vii.   If my body dies, let my body die but don't let my country die.

viii.   One around alone can easily be broken but many around are indestructible.

ix.   I will rule them by fixed laws so that rest and happiness shall prevail in the world.

x.   The merit of an action lies in finishing it to the end.

xi.   Remember you have no companions but your shadow.

xii. As long as you brothers support one another and render assistance to one another, your enemies can never gain the victory over you.

xiii. It will be easy to forget your vision purpose. Once you have fine clothes, fast horses and beautiful women.

RUMI

Persian poet (1207- 1273 AD)

Quotations:

i. Do not feel lonely,

the entire universe is inside you....!!

ii. Love which is based on just a pretty face is not true love, it ends in sheer disgrace.

iii. I said, "Show me the ladder that I may climb up to heaven." He said, "Your head is the ladder, bring your head down under your feet".

iv. We all face death in the end, but on the way, be careful never to hurt a human heart.

v. We are born of love; love is our mother.

vi. Being a candle is not easy; in order to give light one must burn first.

vii. If you are looking for a friend who is faultless, you will be friendless.

viii. Be grateful for whoever comes because each has been sent as a guide from beyond.

ix. Silence is an ocean, speech is a river; when the ocean is searching for you, don't walk into the river, listen to the ocean.

x. Raise your words, not your voice. It is rain that grows flowers, not thunder.

xi. Friendship of the wise is good; wise enemy is better than a foolish friend.

xii. Why do you stay in prison when the door is wide open?

xiii. Beauty surrounds us but usually we need to be walking in a garden to know it.

xiv. Reason is powerless in the expression of love.

xv. Peaceful is the one who is not concerned with having more or less.

xvi. You were born with wings. Why prefer to crawl through life?

xvii. Yesterday I was clever, so I wanted to change the world. Today I am wise, so I am changing myself.

xviii. We carry inside us the wonders we seek outside us.

xix. The only lasting beauty, is the beauty of the heart.

xx. Your heart knows the way, run in that direction.

xxi. Love is a bridge between you and everything.

xxii. The very center of your heart is where the life begins the most beautiful place on earth.

xxiii. The beauty you see in me is a reflection of you.

xxiv. I looked in temples, churches and mosques but I found the divine in my heart.

xxv. Die before you die.

xxvi. There is a voice that does not use words – listen.

xxvii. Love risks everything and asks for nothing.

xxviii.	The desire to know your own soul will end all other desires.
xxix.	Half of life is lost in charming others, the other half is lost in going through anxieties censed by others; leave this play, you have played enough.
xxx.	The cast of knowledge is knowing what to ignore.
xxxi.	I once had a thousand desires, but in my one desire to know "YOU" all other desires melted away.
xxxii.	ALI (as), in bravery you are the lion of your Lord, and in generosity who indeed knows who you are?
xxxiii.	Silence is the correct form of reply.
xxxiv.	Your heart is the size of an ocean. Go find yourself in its hidden depths.
xxxv.	I said to God I will not die before I know you; God replied "he who knows me never dies."
xxxvi.	Love is a bridge between you and everything.
xxxvii.	Why are you so afraid of silence? Silence is the root of everything.
xxxviii.	Purify yourself and become dust, so that from dust followers can grow.
xxxix.	The fault you see in your brother is really in you; the world is a mirror.
xl.	Don't go with the flow. Be the flow.
xli.	If you really trust in God, then work hard, sow the seed and lean of the Almighty help.

xlii.   Maybe you are searching among the branches, for what only appears in the roots.

xliii.   You are not a drop in the ocean,
    You are the entire ocean in a drop.

xliv.   In every religion there is love, yet love has no religion.

xlv.   The lamps are different, but the light is the same.

xlvi.   When we practice loving kindness and compassion, we are the first ones to profit.

xlvii.   What comes, will go, what is found, will be lost again. But what you are is beyond coming and going and beyond description. You are it.

xlviii.   Don't knock on the doors of ordinary houses. Yours arms are long enough to reach the door of heaven.

xlix.   Every person's value is in the thought they hold.

l.   If you want to win hearts, sow the seeds of love.

li.   If you want heaven, stop scattering thorns on the road.

lii.   Be patient when you sit in the dark the dawn is coming.

liii.   The art of knowing is knowing what to ignore.

liv.   Those who don't want to change let them sleep.

lv.   Don't you know yet? It is your light that lights the worlds.

lvi.   When you are the face of anger look behind it and you will find the place of pride.

lvii. Doing as others told me, I was blind. Coming when others calling me, I was lost. Then I left everyone, myself as well. Then I found everyone, myself as well.

lviii. One night I asked love "Tell me truly; who are you?" It said "I am life eternal, I multiply the lovely life".

lix. There are no rules of worship, he will hear the voice of every heart that is sincere.

lx. I lost everything; I have found myself.

lxi. If your tongue thought is a rose, you are a rose garden.

lxii. You are searching the world for treasure, but real treasure is yourself.

lxiii. Once you conquer your selfish self, all your darkness will change to light.

lxiv. You went out in search of gold far and wide, but all along you were gold on the inside.

lxv. People will forget our 1000 good deeds for our 1 fault. Allah (God) will forgive your 1000 bad deeds for one good deed.

NICCOLO MACHIAVELLI

Italian political philosopher

(1469 - 1527)

Quotations:

i. Who so ever desires constant success must change his conduct with the times.

ii. He who wishes to be obeyed must know how to command.

iii. It is better to be feared than loved if you cannot be both.

iv. Of mankind we may say in general they are fickle, hypocritical and greedy of gain.

v. Man should be either treated generously or be destroyed because they take revenge for slight injuries - for heavy ones they cannot.

vi. It is double pleasure to deceive the deceiver.

vii. The first method for estimating the intelligence of a ruler is to look at the men he has around him.

viii. If an injury has to be done to a man it should be so severe that his vengeance need not to be feared.

ix. The new ruler must determine all injuries that he will need to inflict. He must inflict them once and for all.

GURU NANAK

The founder of Sikhism (1469 - 1539)

Quotations:

  i.   Conquer your mind and conquer the world.

  ii.   Before becoming a Muslim, a Hindu, a Sikh or a Cristian, let's become a human first.

  iii.   With your hands carve out your own destiny.

  iv.   Those who have loved are those that have found God.

  v.   The highest religion is to rise to universal brotherhood; aye to consider all creatures your equals.

  vi.   Truth is the highest virtue, but highest still is truthful living.

  vii.   Speak only that which will bring you honor.

  viii.   Only fools argue whether to eat meat or not. They don't understand truth nor do they meditate on it. Who can define what is meat and what is plant? Who knows where the sin lies, being a vegetarian or a non-vegetarian?

  ix.   Do not wish evil for others. Do not speak ill of others. Do not obstruct anyone's activities.

  x.   Emotional attachment to Maya is very painful, this is a bad bargain.

xi.   Life is not about being rich, being popular, being highly educated or being perfect. It is about being real, being humble and being kind.

xii. Easy is to judge the mistakes of others. Difficult is to recognize our own mistakes.

xiii. Luxury and lies have huge maintenance costs. But truth and simplicity are self-maintained without any cost.

xiv. Everything you want someone else has. Make something no one else has.

xv.   When you have money in your hand, you forget who you are. When you don't have money in your hand, the whole world forgets who you are. That's life.

xvi. I don't trust words, I trust actions. People can tell you anything but actions tell you everything.

xvii. When you are a good person, you don't lose people. They lose you.

GALILEO GALILEI

Italian polymath (1564 - 1642)

Quotations:

  i.   All truths are easy to understand once they are discovered; the point is to discover them.

  ii.   You cannot teach a man anything; you can only help him find it within himself.

  iii.   Mathematics is the language with which God has written the universe.

  iv.   The bible shows the way to go to heaven, not the way the heavens go.

  v.   Measure what is measurable and make measurable what is not so.

  vi.   In questions of science, the authority of a thousand is not worth the humble to be reasoning of a single individual.

  vii.   I have never met a man so ignorant that I could not learn something from him.

  viii.   Where the senses fail us, reason must step in.

  ix.   Knowing thyself, that is the greatest wisdom.

  x.   Nature's great book is written in mathematics.

  xi.   God is known by nature in his works and by doctrine in his revealed word.

xii.   I do not feel obliged to believe that the same God who has endowed us with sense, reason and intellect has intended us to forego their use.

xiii. Passion is the genesis of genius.

xiv.   Scripture is the genesis of genius.

xv.   Two truths cannot contradict one another.

WILLIAM SHAKESPEARE

English playwright, poet and actor

(1564 - 1616)

Quotations:

  i.   That do not love that do not show their love.

 ii.   My crown is called content, a crown that seldom kings enjoy.

iii.   When sorrow comes, they come not singles spies but in battalion.

 iv.   Talking is not doing, it is a kind of good deed to say well and yet words are not deeds.

  v.   Desire of having is the sin of carelessness.

 vi.   To do a great right do a little wrong.

vii.   Poor and content is rich and rich enough.

viii. We know what we are but know not what we may be.

 ix.   What is in a name? That which we call a rose by any other name would smell sweet.

  x.   Fish live in the sea, as men do on land, the great ones eat up the little ones.

 xi.   Life every man holds dear but the dear man holds honor far more precious than dear life.

xii.   Speak low, if you speak love.

xiii. As he was valiant, I honor him but as he was ambitious, I slew him.

xiv. Some are born great, some achieve greatness and some have greatness thrust upon them.

xv. Love all, trust few, do wrong to none.

xvi. There is nothing either good or bad but thinking makes it so.

xvii. It is not in the stars to hold our destiny but in ourself.

xviii. Listen to many, speak to a few.

xix. Cowards die many times before their death. The valiant never taste death but once.

xx. All that glitters is not gold.

xxi. You say you love rain, but you open your umbrella; you say you love the sun but you find a shadow spot; you say you love wind but you close your windows. This is why I am afraid when you say you love me.

xxii. Love me or hate me. Both are in my favor…
if you love me I'll always be in your heart…
If you hate me, I'll always be in your mind.

ISAAC NEWTON (1642 – 1726/27)

English mathematician, physicist, astronomer, alchemist, theologian, and author.

Quotations:

   i.   If I have ever made any valuable discoveries, it has been due more to patient attention, than to any other talent.

   ii.   You have to make the rules, not follow them.

  iii.   Every action has an equal and opposite reaction.

  iv.   Gravity explains the motion of the planets, but it cannot explain who sets the planets in motion.

   v.   Live your life as an exclamation rather than an explanation.

  vi.   If I have seen further than others, it is by standing upon the shoulders of giants.

 vii.   Truth is ever to be found in the simplicity, and not in the multiplicity and confusion of things. We build too many wells and not enough bridges.

viii.   If I am anything, which I highly doubt, I have made myself so by hard work.

  ix.   Plato is my friend; Aristotle is my friend; but my greatest friend is truth.

x.   I can calculate the motion of heavenly bodies but not the madness of people.

xi.   Tact is the art of making a point without making an enemy.

xii.   What we know is a drop, what we don't know is an ocean.

xiii.   To myself I am only a child playing on the beach while the ocean of truth lies undiscovered.

xiv.   What goes up must come down.

EDMUND BURKE

Irish born British Statesman

(1729 – 1797)

Quotations:

i.   Our patience will achieve more than our force.

ii.   The only thing necessary for the triumph of evil is for good men to do nothing.

iii.   Those who don't know history are destined to repeat it.

iv.   All tyranny needs to gain a foothold is for people of good conscience to remain silent.

v.   The greater the power, the more dangerous the pause.

vi.   Good order is the foundation of all things.

vii.   Slavery is a weed that grows on every soil.

viii. People will not look forward to posterity, who never look backward to their ancestors.

ix.   To read without reflecting is like eating without digesting.

x.   Sin has many tools but lie is the handle which fits them all.

xi.   Nobody makes a greater mistake than he who did nothing because he could do only a little.

xii.   Education is the cheap defence of nations.

xiii. One that confounds good and evil is an enemy of good.

xiv.   Nothing turns out to be so oppressive and unjust as a feeble government.

xv.   Flattery corrupts both the receiver and the giver.

GEORGE WASHINGTON

The first president of the United States

(1732- 1799)

Quotations:

   i.   It is better to be alone than in bad company.

   ii.   The harder the conflict, the greater the triumph.

   iii.   99% of failures come from people who make excuses.

   iv.   The constitution is the guide which I will never abandon.

   v.   Worry is the interest paid by those who borrow trouble.

   vi.   In time of peace prepare for war.

   vii.   Good moral character is the first essential in man.

   viii.   Example whether it be good or bad, has a powerful influence.

   ix.   Education is the key to unlock the golden door of freedom.

   x.   Where there is no vision there is no hope.

   xi.   If the freedom of speech is taken away then dumb and silent we may be led, like sheep to the slaughter.

   xii.   It is better to offer no excuse than a bad one.

   xiii.   Let your discourse with men of business be short and comprehensive.

   xiv.   A sensible woman can never be happy with a fool.

   xv.   Observe good faith and justice towards all nation and cultivate peace and harmony with all.

THOMAS JEFFERSON

American founding father (1743 - 1826)

Quotations:

i. In matters of style, swim with the current; in matters of principle stand like a rock.

ii. Do you want to know who you are? Don't ask. Act! Action will define you.

iii. Honesty is the first chapter in the book of wisdom.

iv. I cannot live without books.

v. Be polite to all but intimate with a few.

vi. I find that the harder I work, the more luck I seem to have.

JOHAN WOLFGANG VON GOETHE

German poet (1749 - 1832)

Quotations:

i. Power should act and not talk.

ii. What a man does not understand, he does not possess.

iii. Generosity wins favour for every one especially when it is accompanied by modesty.

iv. A useless life is an early death.

v. Which is the best government? That which teaches us to govern ourselves.

vi. Everybody wants to be somebody; nobody wants to grow.

vii. Wisdom lies only in truth.

viii. Common sense is the genius of humanity.

ix. Life teaches us to be less harsh with ourselves and with others.

x. There is nothing in the world more shameful than establishing oneself on lies and fables.

xi. Nothing is more terrible than ignorance in action.

xii. The written word has this advantage that it lasts and can await the time when it is allowed to take effect.

xiii. Nothing is more terrible than ignorance in action.

xiv. Man would not be the finest creature in the world if he were not too fine for it.

92

xv.   One must be something in order to do something.

xvi.   Whoever wishes to keep a secret must hide the fact that he possesses one.

xvii. Ignorant people raise questions which were answered by the wise thousands of years ago.

xviii. He who possesses art and science has religion, he who does

not possess them needs religion.

xix.   One is never deceived but rather deceives oneself.

WILLIAM BLAKE

English poet and the "prophet" of the English

literature   (1757 - 1827)

Quotations:

i.   You never know what is enough, unless you know what is more than enough.

ii. It is easier to forgive an enemy than to forgive a friend.

iii. The most sublime act is to set another before you.

iv. How can a bird that is born for joy, sit in a cage, sing?

v.   No bird soars too high, if he soars with his own wings.

FRIEDRICH VON SCHILLER

German poet (1759 - 1805)

Quotations:

i.   Keep true to the dream of thy youth.

ii.   Appearance rules the world.

iii.   Grace is the beauty of form under the influence of freedom.

iv.   Man only plays when in the full meaning of the word he is man and he is only completely a man when he plays.

v.   The voice of majority is no proof of justice.

vi.   Happy is he who learns to bear what he cannot change.

vii.   To save all we must risk all.

NAPOLEON BONAPARTE

French Military Leader (1769 - 1821)

Quotations:

i. Impossible is a word to be found only in the dictionary of fools.

ii. Religion is what keeps the poor from murdering the rich.

iii. Soldiers generally win battles; generals get credit for them.

iv. He who knows how to flatter, also knows how to slander.

v. Women are nothing but machines of producing children.

vi. Imagination governs the world.

vii. The future destiny of a child is always the work of the mother.

viii. If you want one thing done well, do it yourself.

ix. Show me a family of readers and I will show you the people who move the world.

x. History is a set of lies agreed upon.

xi. A picture is worth a 1000 words.

xii. The best way to keep one's word is not to give it.

xiii. Imagination governs the world.

xiv. As a rule, it is circumstances that make men.

xv. Religion is excellent stuff for keeping common people quite.

xvi. The best cure for body is a quiet mind.

xvii. He who fears being conquered is sure of defeat.

xviii. A leader is a dealer in hope.

xix. History is written by the winners.

xx. Courage is not having the strength to go on, it is going on when you don't have the strength.

xxi. In politics stupidity is not a handicap.

xxii. You must not fight 100 out of ten with one enemy. Or you will teach him all your art of war.

xxiii. One must change one's tactics every 10 years if one wishes to maintain one's superiority.

xxiv. Men are moved by two levers only: Fear and self-interest.

ARTHUR SCHOPENHAUER

German philosopher (1788- 1860)

Quotations:

i. Riches, one may say, are like sea water; the more you drink the thirstier you become, and the same is true of fame.

ii. Two enemies of human happiness are pain and boredom.

iii. Life without pain has no meaning.

iv. Great men are like eagles and build their nests on some lofty solitude.

v. Fame is something which must be won, honor is something which must not be lost.

vi. It would be a good thing to buy the books if one could also buy the time in which to read them.

vii. Reading is thinking with someone else's head instead of one's own.

viii. Only loss teaches us about the value of things.

ix. Talent hits a target no one else can hit; genius hits a target no one else can see.

x. Man are by nature merely indifferent to one another but women are by nature enemies.

xi. To free a man from error is to give and not to take away.

xii. Intellect is invisible to the man who has none.

xiii.   Politeness is to human nature what warmth is to wise.

xiv.   A man can do what he wants, but not want what he wants.

xv.   After your death you will be what you were before your birth.

RALPH WALDO EMERSON

American philosopher (1803 - 1882)

Quotations:

i.   Life is a journey not a destination.

ii.   The purpose of life is not to be happy, it is to be useful and
       honorable, to be compassionate, to have it make some
       difference that you have lived and lived well.

iii.   People only see what they are prepared to see.

iv.   Beauty without the grace is the hook without the bait.

v.   A great man is always willing to be little.

vi.   A man in debt is so far a slave.

vii.   An ounce of action is worth a ton of theory.

viii. Before we acquire great power we must acquire wisdom to
       use it well.

ix.   Every man is a consumer and ought to be a producer.

x.   A man is usually more careful of his money that he is of his
       principles.

xi.   The fox has many tricks, the hedgehog has one but that is the
       best of all.

xii.   What lies behind us and what lies before us are tiny matters
       compared to what lies within us.

xiii. Fear defeats more people than any other thing in the world.

xiv. The creation of a thousand forests is in one acorn.

xv. Patience and fortitude conquer all things.

xvi. The only person you are destined to become is to be the person you decided to be.

xvii. Sorrow looks back, worry looks around, faith looks up.

xviii. It is not the length of life but the depth.

xix. For every minute you are angry you lose sixty seconds of happiness.

xx. Shallow men believe in luck or in circumstances, strong men believe in cause and effect.

xxi. Every artist was first an amateur.

xxii. Let us be silent; we may never hear the whisper of God.

xxiii. If we encounter a man of rare intellect we should ask him the books he read.

NATHANIEL HAWTHORNE

American novelist (1804 - 1864)

Quotations:

i. Time flies over us but leaves its shadow behind.

ii. Easy reading is damn hard writing.

iii. Life is made up of marble and mud.

iv. A hero cannot be a hero unless in a heroic world.

v. Books are as useful to a stupid person as a mirror is useful to a blind person.

vi. A woman's chastity consists like an onion, of a series of coats.

vii. Every individual has a place to fill in the world and it is important in some respect whether he chooses to be so or not.

viii. A pure hand needs no glove to cover it.

ABRAHAM LINCOLN

American statesman – 16th President of
the United States (1809 - 1865)

Quotations:

   i.   Whatever you are, be a good one.

   ii.   I am a slow walker but I never walk back.

  iii.   Life is hard but so very beautiful.

  iv.   Every man's happiness is his own responsibility.

   v.   It is not the years in your life that count; it is the life in your years.

  vi.   Commitment is what transforms a promise into reality.

 vii. Nothing will divert me from my purpose.

viii. Be sure you put your feet in the right place, then stand firm.

  ix.   Those who look for the bad in people will surely find it.

   x.   I would rather be a little nobody than to be an evil somebody.

  xi.   Sir, my concern is not whether God is on our side; my greatest concern is to be on God's side. For God is always right.

 xii. Do I not destroy my enemies when I make them my friends?

xiii. The best way to destroy an enemy is to make him a friend.

xiv. Discipline is choosing between what you want now and what you want most.

xv.   If friendship is your weakest point, then you are the strongest person in the world.

xvi.   You can tell the greatness of a man by what makes him angry.

xvii.   I have always found that mercy bears richer fruits than strict justice.

xviii.   I am not bound to win but I am bound to be true.

xix.   The best way to predict your future is to create it.

xx.   If you want to test a man's character give him power.

xxi.   Government of the people, by the people, for the people, shall not perish from the earth.

xxii.   The ballot is stronger than the bullet.

xxiii.   No man is good enough to govern another man without the others' consent.

xxiv.   Everybody likes a compliment.

xxv.   Important principle may and must be inflexible.

xxvi.   That some achieve great success, is proof to all that others can achieve it too.

xxvii.   Whenever I hear anyone arguing for slavery, I feel a strong impulse to see it tried on him personally.

xxviii.   You can fool some of the people all the time and all people some of the time but you cannot fool all of the people all the time.

SOREN KIERKEGAARD

Danish philosopher (1813- 1855)

Quotations:

i.   The function of prayer is not to influence God, but rather to change the nature of the one who prays.

ii. There are two ways to be fooled, one is to believe what is not true, the other in to refuse to believe what is true.

iii. Do not forget to love yourself.

iv. Life is not a problem to be solved, but reality to be experienced.

v.   Our life always expresses the result of our dominant thoughts.

vi. The tyrant dies and his rule is over; the martyr dies, and his rule begins.

vii. Life can only be understood backwards but it must be lived forwards.

viii. Patience is necessary, and one cannot reap immediately where one has sown.

ix. During the first period of a man's life the greatest danger is not to take the risk.

FYODOR DOSTOYEVSKY

Russian writer (1821 -1888)

Quotations:

i. Man only likes to count his troubles; he does not calculate his happiness.

ii. There is no subject so old that something new cannot be said about it.

iii. Lying to ourselves is more deeply engraved than lying to others.

iv. Men reject their prophets and slay them but they love their martyrs and honor those whom they have slain.

v. The best definition of man is a being that walks on two legs and is ungrateful.

vi. But how could you live and have no story to tell?

vii. To live without hope is to cease to live.

viii. Nothing in the world is harder than speaking the truth and nothing easier than flattery.

ix. It takes something more than intelligence to act intelligently.

ANDREW CARNEGIE

Scottish-American Industrialist

(1835 - 1919)

Quotations:

   i.   No man will make a great leader who wants to do it all himself or get all the credit for doing it.

   ii.   It is the mind that makes the body rich.

   iii.   There is little success where there is little laughter.

   iv.   The man who dies rich dies disgraced.

   v.   No man can become rich without himself enriching others.

   vi.   Aim for the highest.

   vii.   As I grow older I pay less attention to what men say, I just watch what they do.

   viii.   He that cannot reason is a fool, he that will not is a bigot, he that dares not is a slave.

   ix.   Do real and permanent good in this world.

THOMAS HARDY

English novelist and poet (1840 - 1928)

Quotations:

i.   Time changes everything except something within us which is always surpassed by change.

ii.   That man silence is wonderful to listen to.

iii.   A lover without indiscretion is no lover at all.

iv.   Do not do an immoral thing for moral reasons.

v.   The main object of religion is not to get a man into heaven but to get heaven into him.

vi.   Fear is the mother of foresight.

vii.   And yet to every bad there is a worse.

viii.   There is a condition worse than loneliness and that is seeing something that isn't there.

WILLIAM JAMES

American philosopher (1842 - 1910)

Quotations:

i.   To change ones' life, start immediately, do it flamboyantly.

ii.   The greatest weapon against stress is our ability to choose one thought over another.

iii.   Action may not bring happiness but there is no happiness without action.

iv.   There is one cause of human failure and that is man's lack of faith in his true self.

v.   To study the abnormal is the best way of understanding the normal.

vi.   Begin to be now what you will be hereafter.

vii.   The art of becoming wise is the art of knowing what to overlook.

viii.   Pessimism leads to weakness, optimism leads to power.

ix.   If you can change your mind you can change your life.

x.   The great use of life is to spend it for something that will outlast it.

xi.   The aim of a college education is to teach you to know a good man when you see one.

xii.   Anything you may hold firmly in your imagination can be yours.

xiii.   I will act as if what I do makes a difference.

xiv.   When you have to make a choice and don't make it, that is in itself a choice.

xv.   The greatest discovery of any generation is that a human being can alter his life by altering his attitude.

FRIEDRICH NIETZSCHE

German philosopher (1844 - 1900)

Quotations:

i. It is true we love life; not because we want to live but because we are wont to love.

ii. He who cannot give anything away cannot feel anything either.

iii. What is done out of love always takes place beyond good and evil.

iv. Whoever has not got a good father should procure one.

v. To talk much about oneself may also be means of concealing one self.

vi. Not joy but joyness is the mother of debauchery.

vii. You look up when you wish to be exalted and I look down because I am exalted.

viii. Everything the state says is a life and everything it has, it has stolen.

ix. I am not upset that you lied to me, I am upset that from now on I cannot believe you.

VINCENT VAN GOGH

Dutch painter (1853- 1890)

Quotations:

   i.   I would rather die of passion than boredom.

   ii.   The fisherman knows that sea is dangerous and the storm is terrible but they have not found these dangers sufficient reason for remaining ashore.

   iii.   The sadness will last forever.

   iv.   If you truly love nature, you will find beauty everywhere.

   v.   If I am worth anything later; I am worth something now, for wheat is wheat even if people think it is a grass in the beginning.

   vi.   I wish they would take me as I am.

   vii.   I am still far from being what I want to be, but with God's help I shall succeed.

   viii.   I am such a nobody.

   ix.   It must be good to die in the knowledge that one has done some truthful work and to know that as a result one will live on the memory of at least a few and leave a good example for those who come after.

OSCAR WILDE

rish poet and playwright (1854 - 1900)

Quotations:

i.   No man is rich enough to buy his past.

ii.   I am no young enough to know everything.

iii. Be yourself; everyone else is already taken.

iv.   Experience is one thing you can't get for nothing.

v.   True friends stab you in the front.

vi.   Men always want to be a women's first love,
      women like to be a man's last romance.

GEORGE BERNARD SHAW

Irish playwright, critic and political activist (1856 - 1950)

Quotations:

i.   Life is not about finding yourself. Life is about creating yourself.

ii. Progress is impossible without change and those who cannot change their minds cannot change anything.

iii. Where there is no religion, hypocrisy becomes good taste.

iv. Do not try to live forever; you will not succeed.

v.   We learn from history that we learn nothing from history.

vi. Men are wise not by the recollection of our past but by the responsibility for our future.

vii. There is something that holds us together; something that has no word "Love, Love, Love".

viii. Take care to get what you like or you will be forced to live with what you get.

ix. I hear you say why? Always why? You see things and you say why? But I dream things that never were, I say why not?

x.   I often quote myself, it adds spice to my conversation.

THEODORE ROOSEVELT

American politician (1858 - 1919)

Quotations:

i. Believe you can and you are half way there.

ii. Comparison is the thief of joy.

iii. When you play, play hard; when you work, don't play at all.

iv. Whenever you are asked if you can do a job, tell them certainly and then get busy to find out how to do it.

v. Knowing what is right doesn't mean much unless you do what is right.

vi. All the resources we need are in the mind.

vii. Nine-tenths of wisdom is being wise in time.

viii. People ask the difference between a leader and a boss. The leader leads and the boss drives.

ix. In any moment of decision, the best thing you can do is the right thing, the next best thing is the wrong thing and the worst thing is do nothing.

RABINDRANATH TAGORE

First Noble prize winner

(non- European) in literature

(1861 - 1941)

Quotations:

i. You cannot cross the sea merely by standing and staring at the water.

ii. I slept and dreamt that life was joy,

   I awoke and saw that life was service,

   I acted and behold, service was joy.

iii. It is very simple to be happy, but it is very difficult to be simple.

iv. Facts are many but truth is one.

v. Depth of friendship doesn't depend on the length of acquaintance.

vi. The roots below the earth claim no rewards for making the branches fruitful.

vii. Don't limit a child to your own learning for he was born in a different time.

SWAMI VIVEKANAND

Great philosopher and spiritual leader

(1863 - 1902)

Quotations:

i. Talk to yourself once a day, otherwise you may miss meeting

   an excellent person in the world.

ii. Strength is life; weakness is death.

iii. Struggle is the sign of life.

iv. He who struggles is better that he who never attempts.

v. Prayer is not an attempt to change God's mind, but it's an attempt to let God change our mind.

vi. Arise. Awake. And stop not until goal is achieved.

vii. Can't you wear proper clothes to be a gentleman.

viii. In your culture dress makes gentlemen but in our culture character makes gentlemen.

ix. All power is within you; you can do anything and everything.

x. If I love myself despite my infinite faults, how can I hate anyone at the glimpse of a few faults?

xi. You cannot believe in God unless you believe in yourself.

xii. See for the highest, aim for the highest and you shall reach the highest.

xiii. Relationships are more important than life but it is important for relationships to have life in them.

xiv. The only definition that can be given of morality is this: that which is selfish is immoral and that which is unselfish is moral.

xv. If a mind is intensely eager, everything can be accomplished; mountains can be crumbled with atoms.

xvi. In a conflict between the heart and the brain, follow your heart.

xvii. Your beliefs don't make you a better person, your behavior
does.

xviii. Let us work without desire for name or fame or rule over the others.

xix. The greatest religion is to be true to your nature, have faith in yourselves.

xx. There is only one difference between dreams and aim. Dream requires effortless sleep and aim requires sleepless efforts. Sleep for dreams and wake up for aims.

xxi. My motto is to learn whatever good things I may come across anywhere.

xxii. The man who says he has nothing more to learn is already at his last grasp.

xxiii. As long as I live, so do I learn.

xxiv. We want the education by which character is formed, strength of mind is increased, the intellect is expanded and by which one can stand on one's own feet.

xxv. When an idea exclusively occupies the mind, it is transformed into an actual physical or mental state.

xxvi. One ounce of practice is worth a thousand pounds of theory.

MAHATMA GANDHI

Anti- colonial and Indian ethicist

(1869 - 1948)

Quotations:

i. Relationships are based on four principles: respect, understanding, acceptance and appreciation.

ii. Poverty is the worst form of violence.

iii. Honest disagreement is often a good sign of progress.

iv. Justice that loves gives in surrender, justice that law gives in a punishment?

v. Earth provides enough to satisfy every man's needs but not every man's greed.

vi. Truth is one, paths are many.

vii. The weak can never forgive, forgiveness is the attribute of the strong.

viii. The best way to find your self is to lose yourself in the service of others.

ix. Live as if you were to die tomorrow. Learn as if you were to live forever.

x. Man becomes great exactly in the day in which he works for the welfare of his fellow men.

xi. You can change me, you can torture me, you can even destroy this body, but you will never impression my mind.

xii. Anger and intolerance are the enemies of correct understanding.

xiii. An ounce of practice is worth more than a ton of preaching.

xiv. Be the change you want to see in the world.

xv. In a gentle way, you can shake the world.

xvi. The future depends on what we are in the present.

xvii. Where there is love, there is life.

xviii. It is health that is real wealth; not pieces of gold and silver.

xix. A man is the product of his thoughts; what he thinks, he becomes.

xx. Anger and intolerance are the enemies of correct understanding.

xxi. An eye for an eye only ends up making the whole world blind.

xxii. I will not let anyone walk through my mind with their dirty feet.

xxiii. Happiness is when what you think, what you say and what you do are in harmony.

xxiv. In prayer it is better to have a heart without words than words without a heart.

xxv. Prayer is the key of the morning and the bolt of the evening.

xxvi. Before the throne of the almighty, man will be judged not by his acts but by his intentions.

xxvii. Anger is the enemy of non-violence and pride is a monster that swallows it up.

xxviii. Nobody can hurt me without my permission.

xxix. To believe in something and not to live it is dishonest.

xxx. You must be the change you wish to see in the world.

THOMAS MANN

German novelist (1875 - 1955)

Quotations:

i. It is love, not reason that is stronger than death.

ii. Tolerance becomes a crime when applied to Evil.

iii. A great truth is a truth whose opposite is also truth.

MOHAMMED ALI JINNAH

The founder of Pakistan (1876 - 1948)

Quotations:

i.   I do not believe in taking the right decision. I take a decision and make it right.

ii.   It is faith that makes people afraid of meeting challenges and I believe in myself.

iii. Think a hundred times before you take a decision, but once that decision is taken stand by it as one man.

iv.   No nation can rise to the height of glory unless your women are side by side with you.

v.   My message to you all is of hope, courage and confidence.

vi.   Democracy is on the blood of the Muslims,

    a.   who looks upon complete equality of mankind.

    b.   And believe in fraternity, equality and liberty.

vii. Expect the best, prepare for the worst.

viii. India is not a nation, nor a country. It is a subcontinent of nationalities.

ix.   Failure is a word unknown to me.

x.   No struggle can ever succeed without women participating side by side with men.

124

xi.   There are two powers in the world; one is the sword and

xii.   the other is the pen. There is a great competition and rivalry between the two. There is a third power stronger than both of them; that is women.

xiii. Think before selecting your leader and when you have selected him follow him, but in case you find his policy detrimental to your interests kick him out.

ALBERT EINSTEIN

German theoretical physicist

(1879 - 1955)

Quotations:

i.   Information is not knowledge.

ii.   Only a life lived for others is worth living.

iii.   Never do anything against conscience even if the state demands it.

iv.   Try not to become a man of success but rather to become a man of value.

v.   If you can't explain it simply, you don't understand it well enough.

vi.   Imagination is more important than knowledge.

vii.   Logic will get you from A to B. Imagination will take you everywhere.

viii.   If you want to live a happy life, tie it to a goal; not to people or objects.

ix.   Education is what remains after one has forgotten everything he learned in school.

x.   Education is not the learning of facts but the training of the mind to think.

xi. The world will not be destroyed by those who do evil but by those who watch them without doing anything.

xii. Try not to become a man of success but rather try to become a man of value.

xiii. Life is like riding a bicycle, to keep your balance you must keep moving.

xiv. Once you stop learning, you start dying.

xv. What is right is not always popular and what is popular is not always right.

xvi. I speak to everyone in the same way whether he is the garbage man or the President of the university.

xvii. Stay away from negative people; they have a problem with every solution.

xviii. A clever person solves a problem. A wise person avoids it.

xix. Weak people revenge, strong people forgive, intelligent people ignore.

xx. The only thing more dangerous than ignorance is arrogance.

xxi. Weakness of attitude becomes weakness of character.

xxii. If people are good only because they take punishment and hope for reward, then we are a sorry lot indeed.

xxiii. Once we accept our limits we go beyond them.

xxiv. Less knowledge - big ego.
       More knowledge - less ego.

xxv. Learn from yesterday, live for today, hope for tomorrow.

xxvi.	The only thing that interferes with my learning is my education.
xxvii.	It is harder to crack a prejudice than an atom.
xxviii.	A person who never made a mistake never tried anything new.
xxix.	Why should I memorize the same thing I can easily get from a book?
xxx.	You only fail when you stop trying.
xxxi.	Do not be a slave of your ego.
xxxii.	When lies connect people together, truth eventually separates them.
xxxiii.	Everybody is a genius but if you judge a fish by its ability to climb a tree, it will live its whole life believing that it is stupid.
xxxiv.	The world will not be destroyed by those who do evil, but by those who watch them without doing nothing.

PRESIDENT FRANKLIN D. ROOSEVELT

American politician (1882- 1945)

Quotations:

i. The only thing we have to fear is fear itself.

ii. Speak softly and carry a big stick. You will go far.

iii. The nation that destroys its soul, destroys itself.

iv. Keep your eyes on the stars and your feet on the ground.

v. The only man who never makes a mistake is the man who never does anything.

vi. Do what you can with what you have, where are you?

vii. The most practical kind of politics is the politics of decency.

viii. Repetition does not transform a lie into a truth.

ix. Throughout the world, change is the order of the day.

VIRGINIA WOOLF

English writer (1882 - 1941)

Quotations:

i.   As a woman, I have no country twice,

      As a woman, my country is the whole world.

ii.   Books are the mirrors of the souls.

iii.   Why are women so much more interesting to men than men are to women?

iv.   As long as she thinks of a man no body objects to a woman thinking.

KHALIL GIBRAN OF LEBANON

Lebanese-American writer (1883 - 1931)

Quotations:

i. If the other person injures you, you may forget the injury but if you injure him you will always remember.

ii. Trust in dreams for in them is hidden the gate to eternity.

iii. You may forget with whom you laughed, but you will never forget with whom you wept.

iv. The smallest act of kindness is worth more than the greatest intention.

v. If you love somebody, let them go, for they return, they were always yours and if they don't they never were.

vi. If your heart is a volcano, how shall you expect flowers to bloom?

vii. Beauty is not in the face; beauty is a light in the heart.

viii. We are all prisoners but some of us are in cells with windows and some without.

ix. And God said "love your enemy" and I obeyed him and I loved myself.

x.   One day you will ask me which is more important? My life or yours? I will say mine and you will walk away not knowing that you are my life.

xi.   Sadness is but a wall between two gardens.

xii.   Doubt is a pain too lonely to know that faith is his twin brother.

xiii.   Our worst fault is our preoccupation with faults of others.

xiv.   Love and doubt have never been on speaking terms.

xv.   Life without love is like a tree without fruit.

xvi.   The eye of a human being is a microscope which makes the world seem bigger than it really is.

xvii.   Friendship is always a sweet responsibility; never an opportunity.

xviii.   My point is not your path; yet together we walk hand in hand.

xix.   Listen to the woman when she looks at you not when she talks at you.

xx.   Much of your pain is self-chosen.

xxi.   Rest in reason, move in passion.

xxii.   Progress lies not in enhancing what is but in advancing towards what will be.

xxiii.   To be little you have to be little.

DALE CARNEGIE

American writer and lecturer (1888 – 1955)

Quotations:

i.   Don't be afraid of enemies who attack you. Be afraid of the friends that flatter you.

ii. Talk to someone about themselves and they will listen for hours.

iii. Even God doesn't propose to judge a man till his last days, why should you and I?

iv. Our thoughts make us what we are.

v.   Knowledge isn't power until it is applied.

vi. Be wiser than other people if you can: but do not tell them so.

vii. No matter what happens, always be yourself.

viii. Nothing can bring you peace but yourself.

ix. You can measure the size of a person by what makes him or her angry.

x.   You can make more friends in two months by becoming interested in other people than you can in two years by trying to get other people interested in you.

xi. If you want to conquer fear, don't sit home and think about it. Go out and get busy.

xii. Inaction breeds doubt and fear.

Action breeds confidence and courage.

xiii. The expression a woman wears on her face is far more important than the clothes she wears on her back.

xiv. There are four ways and only four ways in which we have contact with the world, we are evaluated and classified by these four contacts:

   a. What we do,

   b. how we look,

   c. what we say,

   d. how we say it.

xv. Success is getting what you want.

Happiness is wanting what you get.

xvi. Each nation feels superior to other nations; that breeds patriotism and wars.

xvii. If you want to be enthusiastic, act enthusiastic.

xviii. You can conquer almost any fear if you will only make up

your mind to do so, for remember, fear doesn't exist anywhere except in the mind.

xix. Fear not those who argue but those who dodge.

xx. Only the prepared speaker deserves to be confident.

xxi. We all have possibilities we don't know about, we can do things we don't even dream we can do.

PANDIT JAWAHARLAL NEHRU

1st Prime minister of India (1889 - 1964)

Quotations:

i.   It is a fundamental rule of human life that if the approach is good, the response is good.

ii. You can tell the condition of a nation by looking at the status of its women.

iii. Success often comes to those who dare to act; it seldom goes

iv. to the timid who are ever afraid of the consequences.

v.   The person who runs away exposes himself to that very danger more than a person who sits quietly.

vi. The person who talks most of his own virtues is often the least virtuous.

vii. Without peace all other dreams vanish and are reduced to ashes.

viii. Action to be effective must be directed to clearly conceived ends.

ix. There is perhaps nothing so bad and so dangerous in life as fear.

x.   Our chief defect is that we are more given to talking about things than doing things.

DWIGHT D. EISENHOWER

The 34th president of the United States

(1890- 1969)

Quotations:

i. Leadership is the art of getting someone else to do something you want done because he wants to do it.

ii. Pull the string and it will follow wherever you wish. Push it and it will go nowhere at all.

iii. If you want total security, go to prison; there you are fed, clothed, given medical care and so on. The only thing lacking is freedom.

iv. The supreme quality for leadership is unquestionably integrity; without it no real success is possible, no matter whether it is on a section gang, a football field, in an army or in an office.

v. A person that values its priveleges above its principles soon loses both.

vi. Peace and justice are two sides of the same coin.

vii. Plans are nothing, planning is everything.

viii. We seek peace knowing that peace is the climate of freedom.

ix. Unless we progress, we regress.

NORMAN VINCENT PEALE

American Protestant clergyman and author (1898 - 1993)

Quotations:

    i. Change your thoughts and you change your world.

   ii. Whatever you are doing in the game of life, give it all you have got.

  iii. Help other people to cope with their problems and your own will be easier to cope with.

  iv. Who decides whether you shall be happy or unhappy? You do.

   v. One of the basic laws of human existence is: find yourself, know yourself and be yourself.

  vi. I expect the best and with God's help I will attain the best.

 vii. First thing every morning before you arise say out loud, "I believe".

viii. The trouble with most of us is that we would rather be ruined by praise than saved by criticism.

  ix. Four things for success: work and pray, think and believe.

   x. Empty pockets never held anyone back; only empty heads and empty hearts can do that.

  xi. Getting people to like you is merely the other sides of liking them.

 xii. The only people who don't have problems are in a cemetery.

xiii.   God answers prayer in three ways; yes, no and wait a while.

xiv.   Nothing is more confusing than people who give good advice but set a bad example.

JEAN PAUL SARTRE

French philosopher (1905 – 1980)

Quotations:

   i.   Everything has been figured out except how to live.

   ii.   Better to die on one's feet than to live on one's knees.

  iii.   We do not judge the people we love.

  iv.   Politics is a science, you can demonstrate that you are right and others are wrong.

   v.   One cannot become a saint when one works sixteen hours a day.

  vi.   Man is fully responsible for his nature and his choices.

 vii.   Only the guy who isn't rowing has time to rock the boat.

MOTHER TERESA

Roman Catholic nun and missionary
(1910 – 1997)

Quotations:

i. The poor do not need our sympathy and our pity, the poor need our love and compassion.

ii. One of the greatest diseases is to be nobody to anybody.

iii. If you can't feed a hundred people then just feed one.

iv. Peace begins with a smile.

v. I do not pray success, I ask for faithfulness.

vi. What can you do to promote world peace? Go home and love your family.

vii. God does not require us to succeed; he only requires us to try.

viii. If we really want to love, we must learn how to forgive.

ix. Some people come in your life as blessing, some people come in your life as lesson.

x. If you judge people you have no time to love them.

xi. A life not lived for others is not a life.

xii. Life is a challenge, meet it.

Life is beauty, admire it.

Life is duty, complete it.

xiii. It is very easy to give an example but it's very difficult to become an example!!!

xiv. Do things for people not because of who they are or what they do in return, but because of who you are.

xv. Peace begins with a smile.

xvi. We shall never know all the good that a simple smile can do.

JOHN F. KENNEDY

American politician – 35th president of the
United States (1917 – 1963)

Quotations:

i. Mankind must put an end to war before war puts an end to mankind.

ii. My fellow Americans, ask not what your country can do for you, ask what you can do for your country.

iii. A man may die, nations may rise and fall but an idea lives on.

iv. The time to repair the roof is when the sun is shining.

v. Let us never negotiate out of fear but let never fear to negotiate.

vi. The greater our knowledge increases the more our ignorance unfolds.

vii. Forgive your enemies but never forget their names.

viii. Change is the law of life and those who look only to the past

or present are certain to miss the future.

ix. Liberty without learning is always in peril and learning without liberty is always in vain.

x.   A nation that is afraid to let its people judge the truth and falsehood in an open market is a nation that is afraid of its people.

xi.   Do not pray for easy lives, pray for stronger men.

xii.   A child miseducated is a child lost.

xiii.   We must use time as a tool not as a couch.

xiv.   The human mind is a fundamental resource.

xv.   Let us not seek the republican answer or the democratic answer but the right answer.

NELSON MANDELA

Political leader – The first president of South Africa (1918 - 2013)

Quotations:

i. If you talk to a man in a language he understands, that goes to his head; if you talk to him in his language that goes to his heart.

ii. Courageous people do not fear forgiving for the sake of peace.

iii. Give a child love, laughter, and peace; not Aids.

iv. If you are poor, you are not likely to live long.

v. No country can really develop unless its citizens are educated.

vi. Only free men can negotiate; a prisoner cannot enter into contracts.

vii. In countries where innocent people are lying, the leaders are following their blood rather than their brains.

viii. In my country we go to prison first and then become president.

ix. Education is the most powerful weapon which you can use to change the world.

x. It always seems impossible until it's done.

xi. Freedom would be meaningless without security in the home and in the street.

xii. We must use time wisely and forever realize that the time always ripe to do right.

xiii. Where the water starts boiling it is foolish to turn off the heat.

xiv. I cannot pretend that I'm brave and that I can beat the whole world.

xv. A good head and a good heart are always a formidable combination.

xvi. To deny people their human rights is to challenge their very humanity.

xvii. After climbing a great hill, one only funnels that there are many hills to climb.

xviii. If you want to make peace with your enemy you have to work with your enemy; then, he becomes your partner.

xix. A winner is a dreamer who never gives up.

xx. When women are determined, they can overcome anything.

xxi. It is wise to persuade people to do things and make them think it was their own idea.

xxii. I stand here before you not as a prophet, but as a humble servant of you, the people.

xxiii. Real leaders must be able to sacrifice all for the freedom of their people.

HENRY KISSINGER

American politician and author (1923 -)

Quotations:

i.   The task of the leader is to get people from where they are to where they have not begun.

ii. Who controls money, controls the world.

iii. Control oil and you control nations; control food and you control the people.

iv. To be an enemy of America can be dangerous but to be a friend is fatal.

v.   Diplomacy, the art of restraining power.

vi. America has no permanent friends or enemies; only interests.

MARGARET THATCHER

Prime Minister of the United Kingdom from 1979 – 1990 (1925- 2013)

Quotations:

i. If you want something said, ask a man.

   If you want something done, ask a woman.

ii. Each regulation is a restriction of freedom.

   Each regulation has a cost.

iii. Any woman who understands the problem of running a home is very close to understanding the problems of running a country.

iv. Socialism fails when they run out of money of others.

v. Being in the middle of the road is very dangerous, you get hit by traffic both ways.

MALCOLM X

Human rights activist (1925 - 1965)

Quotations:

   i.   The future belongs to those who prepare for it today.

   ii.   If you are not ready to die for it, put the word "freedom" out of your vocabulary.

   iii.   A man who stands for nothing will fall for anything.

   iv.   History proves that the white man is a devil.

   v.   Without education, you're not going anywhere in this world.

   vi.   Truth is on the side of the oppressed.

   vii.   America needs to understand Islam because this is the one religion that erases from its society the race problem.

   viii.   If Africa wasn't beautiful, the white man wouldn't want it.

   ix.   The media's the most powerful entity on earth. They have the power to make the innocent guilty and to make the guilty innocent, and that's power because they control the mind of \the masses.

   x.   When I is replaced by "we", even wiliness becomes wellness.

ZIG ZIGLAR

American author (1926 - 2012)

Quotations:

i. Many marriages would be better if the husband and wife understood that they are on the same side.

ii. You will get all you want in life if you help enough other people get what they want.

iii. Your attitude, not your aptitude, will determine your altitude.

iv. Every choice you make has an end result.

v. A lot of people quit looking for work as soon as they find a job.

vi. Expect the best, prepare for the worst, capitalize on what comes.

vii. A goal properly set is half way reached.

viii. Positive thinking will let you do everything better than negative thinking will.

ix. Remember that failure is an event, not a person.

x. Every obnoxious act is a cry for help.

xi. Rich people have small TVs and big libraries and poor people have small libraries and big TVs.

xii. You don't have to be great to start but you have to start to become great.

xiii. Motivation gets you going and habit gets you there.

xiv.   The greatest of all mistakes is to do nothing because you think you can only do a little.

MARTIN LUTHER KING JR

American activist (1929 – 1968)

Quotations:

    i.   We need leaders not in love with money but in love with justice; not in love with publicity but in love with humanity.

   ii.   We must learn to live together as brothers or we will perish together as fools.

  iii.   We have learned to fly in the air, like birds and swim in the sea like fish, but we have not learned the simple art of living together as brothers.

  iv.   I know that love is ultimately the only answer to mankind's problems.

   v.   As long as the mind is enslaved, the body can never be free.

  vi.   Hatred paralyzes life; love releases it,
Hatred confuses life; love harmonizes it,
Hatred darkens life; love illuminates it.

 vii.   Darkness cannot drive out darkness; only light can do that. Hate cannot drive out hate; only love can do that.

viii.   Injustice anywhere is a threat to justice everywhere.

  ix.   The time is always right, to do what is right.

   x.   Life's most persistent and urgent question is, what are you doing for others?

xi. Our lives begin to end the day we become silent about things that matter.

xii. In the end, we will remember not the words of our enemies but the silence of our friends.

xiii. Love is the only force capable of transforming an enemy into a friend.

xiv. The ultimate tragedy is not the oppression and cruelty by bad people but the silence over that by the good people.

xv. If I cannot do great things, I can do small things in a great way.

xvi. Not everybody can be famous but everybody can be great, because greatness is determined by service.

APJ ABDUL KALAM

The 11th president of India

(1931 - 2015)

Quotations:

i. Leaders think and talk about the solutions.
Followers think and talk about the problems.

ii. Our parents were patient when we were young, now it's our time to be patient during their old age.

iii. Definition of birthday:
the only day in your life… your mother smiled when you cried.

iv. Never complain about the difficulties in life because a director (God) always gives the hardest roles to his best actor.

v. There are two types of pain in this world: pain that hurts you, and pain that changes you.

vi. The best brains of the nation may be found on the last benchesof the classroom.

vii. Let us sacrifice our today so that our children can have a better future.

viii. If we are not free, no one will respect us.

ix. Where there is a rightness in the heart, there is beauty in the character. When there is beauty in the character there is harmony at the home, when there is harmony in the home there is order in the nation. When there is order in the nation, there is peace in the world.

x. Don't take rest after your first victory, because if you fail in the second, more life are waiting to say, that your first victory was just luck.

xi. If you want to shine like a sun, first burn like a sun!

xii. Your best teacher is your last mistake.

xiii. If you salute your duty, you need not to salute anybody. If you pollute your duty, you have to salute everybody.

xiv. Creativity is seeing something but thinking differently.

xv. If you fail, never give up because fail means "first attempt in learning".

xvi. Science is a beautiful gift to humanity; we should not distort it.

xvii. For great men religion is a way of making friends, small people make religion a fighting tool.

xviii. If four things are followed, having a great aim, acquiring a knowledge, hard work and perseverance, then anything can be achieved.

xix. Small aim is a crime; have great aim.

xx. Confidence and hard work is the best medicine to kill the disease called failure; it will make you a successful person.

xxi. War is never a lasting solution for any problem.

xxii. You see God helps only people who work hard; that principle is very clear.

xxiii. Great teachers emanate out of knowledge, passion and compassion.

xxiv. Dreams is not what you see in your sleep, it is the thing which doesn't let you sleep.

xxv. All birds find shelter during a rain, but eagle avoids rain by flying above the clouds. Problems are common but attitude makes a difference.

xxvi. It is very easy to defeat someone but it is very hard to win someone.

xxvii. Behind the parents, stands the school and behind the teacher stands the home.

xxviii. Praise publicly but criticize privately.

xxix. Each individual creature of the beautiful planet is created by God to fulfil a particular role.

xxx. One good book is equal to hundred good friends but one good friend is equal to a library.

xxxi. All of us do not have equal talents. But all of us have equal opportunity to develop our talents.

xxxii. Without your involvement, you cannot succeed, with your involvement you can't fail.

xxxiii. If we are not free no one will respect us.

xxxiv. A teacher should have a creative mind.

xxxv. What is success? When your signature turns into an autograph.

HH THE AGA KHAN

Imam and Aga Khan since 1957. (1936 -)

Quotations:

i. In knowledge society, the most productive investment we can make are investments in education.

ii. As trustees of God's creation, we are instructed to seek to leave the world a better place than it was when we came into it.

iii. Any differences must be resolved through tolerance, through understanding, through compassion, through dialogue, through forgiveness, through generosity, all of which represent ethics of Islam.

iv. Men and women should marry freely with their own choice and that free choice is the highest and holiest of all blessings.

v. Freedom in any area of human activity does not mean the moral license to abuse that freedom.

vi. Progress in ummah means moving forward in quality of life but not giving up your identity, not giving up your value systems; indeed our values system is massively important for the future.

BRUCE LEE

Martial Artist (1940 – 1973)

Quotations:

   i.   If you spend too much time thinking about a thing you will never get it done.

   ii.   Showing off is the fools' idea of glory.

  iii. As you think, so shall you become.

  iv. To know oneself is to study oneself in action with another person.

   v.   Real living is living for others.

  vi. Always be yourself, express yourself, have faith in yourself, do not go out and look for a successful personality and duplicate it.

 vii. Knowledge will give you power but character will give you respect.

viii. If you truly love life, don't waste time.

  ix. To help with circumstances I create opportunities.

   x.   To be trusted is a greater compliment than being loved.

MUHAMMAD ALI

Legendary boxer born on Jan 17, 1942.

Quotations:

i.   If your mind can conceive it and your heart can believe it then you can achieve it.

ii. Service to others is the rent you pay for your room in the heaven.

iii. I don't smoke but I keep a matchbox in my pocket.

iv. When my heart slips towards a sin, I burn a matchstick and heat my palm then I say to myself "Ali, you can't bear even this heat. How would you bear the unbearable heat of hell?"

v.   If you ever dreamed of beating me then you better wake up and apologize.

vi. I am not fighting one man, I am fighting a lot of men; my mission is to bring freedom to 30 million people.

vii. Champions are not made in gyms; champions are made from something they have deep inside them; a desire, a dream, a vision.

viii. A man who views the world the same at 50 as he did at 20 has waisted 30 years of his life.

ix. "I am the greatest"; I said that even before I knew I was.

x.   The man who has no imagination has no wings.

xi. It is hard to be humble, when you are as great as I am.

xii. Silence is golden when you can't think of a good answer.

xiii. I believe in the religion of Islam; I believe in Allah and peace.

xiv. Old age is just a record of one's whole life.

xv. I hated every minute of training, but I said "Don't quit"; suffer now and live the rest of your life as a champion.

xvi. The will must be stronger than the skill.

xvii. The best way of making your dreams come true is to wake up.

xviii. My principles are more important than the money or my title.

xix. I am an ordinary man who worked hard to develop the talent I was given; I believe in myself and I believe in the goodness of others.

xx. If you haven't learned the meaning of friendship, you really haven't learnt anything.

xxi. Live everyday as it were your last because some day you are going to be right.

xxii. We have one life, it soon will be past; what we do for God is that that will last

BILL GATES

American software developer.

Co-founder of Microsoft (1955 -)

Quotations:

   i.   If you are born poor it's not your fault or mistake but if you die poor, it is your mistake.

   ii.   I failed in some subjects in exams but my friend passed in all, now he is an engineer in Microsoft and I am the owner of Microsoft.

   iii.   I chose a lazy person to do a hard job because a lazy person will find an easy way to do it.

   iv.   As we look ahead into the next century, leaders will be those who empower others.

   v.   Life is not fair; get used to it.

   vi.   If you can't make it good, at least make it look good.

   vii.   Do not compare yourself with anyone in this world; if you do so you are insulting yourself.

   viii.   Your most unhappy customer is your greatest source of learning.

BARACK OBAMA

44th President of the United States

(1961 -)

Quotations:

i.   Where you are right now doesn't have to determine where you end up.

ii.   The best way to not feel hopeless is get up and do something.

iii.   Change is never easy but always possible.

iv.   If you are walking down the right path and you are walking to keep walking eventually, you'll make progress.

v.   If you run you stand a chance of losing, but if you don't run you have already lost.

vi.   Cynicism is a sorry kind of wisdom.

vii.   Do not judge.

viii.   Share your happiness.

KURT COBAIN

American Singer (1967- 1994)

Quotations:

i.   I would rather be hated for whom I am than loved for who I am not.

ii. You create attention to attract attention.

iii. We have no right to express an opinion until we know all of the answers.

iv. It is better to burn out than fade away.

v.   I like to complain and do nothing to make things better.

vi. The only wealth in this world is children more than all the money and power on earth.

vii. Wanting to be someone else is a waste of the person you are.

viii. The duty of youth is to challenge corruption.

ix. I am not well read, but when I read I read well.

x.   They laugh at me because I am different.
     I laugh at them because they are all same.

Section 2

Quotations from different religions and proverbs from different countries

Quotations from different religions

Ten Quranic commandments

1. Speak kindly (2:83)
2. Speak the truth (3:17)
3. Speak justice (6:152)
4. Speak graciously (17:23)
5. Speak fairly (17:23)
6. Speak politely (17:53)
7. Speak no lie (22:30)
8. Speak gently (20:44)
9. Speak not in vain (22.3)
10. Speak straight (33:70)

THE HOLY QURAN

- So do not claim yourselves to be pure; he is most knowing who fears him. (Noble Quran 53:32)
- And be good "to others" as god has been good to you (Noble Quran 28:77)
- God knows the treachery of the eyes and all that the hearts of man conceal. (Noble Quran 40:19)
- Judgement Day: He will say "my lord, send me back." (Noble Quran 23:99)
- An ease for me my task. (Noble Quran 20:26)
- Do not insult others by (offensive) nicknames. (Noble Quran 49:11)
- Be nice to people who work under your care. (Noble Quran 4:36)
- Do not expect a return for your good behaviour, not even thanks. (Noble Quran 76:9).
- Men are the protectors and maintainers of women. (Noble Quran 4:34)
- Forgive them even if they are not sorry. (Noble Quran 24:22)
- Allah (alone) is sufficient for us, and he is the best disposer of affairs (for us). (Noble Quran 3:173)

- Whoever does righteous, it is for his (own) soul; and who ever does evil (does so) against it and your lord is not ever unjust to (his) servants. (Noble Quran 41:46)

- Indeed, my protector is Allah (God), who has sent down the book, and he is an ally to the righteous. (Noble Quran 7:196)

- And when you testify be just, even if (it concerns) a near relative. (Noble Quran 6:152)

- No one besides Allah (God) can rescue a soul from hardship. (Noble Quran 53:58)

- What lead you into hell fire? They will say: we were not of those who prayed, nor did we use to feed the poor. (Noble Quran 74: 42)

- My lord, grant me [a child] from among the righteous. (Noble Quran 37:100)

- Indeed, God loves those who rely upon him. (Noble Quran 3:159)

- God never changes the condition of people unless they strive to change themselves. (Noble Quran 13:11)

- Call upon your lode in humility and privately. (Noble Quran 7.55)

- Those or whom you call besides Allah cannot even create a fly. (Noble Quran 22:73)

- No person knows what he will earn tomorrow, and no person knows in what land he will die. (Noble Quran 31:34)

- And you will certainly be questioned about what you used to do. (Noble Quran 16:93)

- And we created you in pairs. (Noble Quran 78:8)

- God says (Allah) "I listen to the prayer of every suppliant when he calls upon me." (Noble Quran 2:186)

The 10 Commandments (Judaism)

1. The Lord, am your God, you shall not have other Gods beside me.

2. You shall not take the name of the Lord, your God in vain.

3. Remember to keep holy the God's Day.

4. Honor your father and your mother.

5. You shall not kill.

6. You shall not commit adultery.

7. You shall not steal.

8. You shall not bear false witness against your neighbors.

9. You shall not covet your neighbor's wife.

10. You shall not covet your neighbor's goods.

LAWS OF KARMA

- How people treat you is their karma, how you react is yours.

- Karma is Karma, Karma is in life; you do the wrong things, you get wrong things out.

- Like gravity, Karma is so basic we often don't even notice it.

- Don't waste your time on revenge, the people who hurt you will eventually face their own karma.

- Karma simply put is an action for an action, good or bad.

- There is a natural law of karma that vindictive people who go out of their way to hurt others will end up broke and alone.

- Karma is like a boomerang, what you give out, will come back to you.

- Do good and good will come to you.

- Before you say anything to anyone, consider how you would feel if that person said the same thing to you.

PROVERBS FROM THE BIBLE

- A fool kreth all his mind: but a wise man keepth it in after words. (29:11 KJV)
- Whoever walks with the wise becomes wise but the companion of fools will suffer harm. (13:20)

Proverbs and sayings from different countries

ENGLISH PROVERBS AND SAYINGS

- It takes two to make a quarrel.
- Early to bed and early to rise, makes a man healthy, wealthy and wise.
- The devil finds work for idle hands.
- It's an ill wind that blows nobody any good.
- The pen is mightier than the swords.
- No news is good news.
- Least said soonest mended.
- Familiarity breeds contempt.
- Still water runs deep.
- Absence makes the heart grow fonder.
- A bad workman always blames his tools.
- Speech is silver, silence is golden.
- Don't judge a book by its cover.
- Too many cooks spoil the broth.
- Do not count chickens before they are hatched.
- If wishes were horses beggars would ride.
- You can lead a horse to water but you can't make him drink.
- Time heels old wounds.
- An ounce of prevention is better than a pound of cure.
- A new broom sweeps clean.

- In the kingdom of the blind the one-eyed man is king.

- A leopard cannot change its spots.

- Laugh and the world laughs with you, cry and you cry alone.

- Children should be seen and not heard.

- Birds of a same feather flock together.

- Two is company, three is crowd.

- Truth is friction than fiction.

- Action speaks louder than words.

- A rolling stone gathers no moss.

- Dead man tells no lies.

- A bird in the hand is worth two in the bush.

- Once bitten twice shy.

- Who keeps company with wolves will learn to howl.

- There is none so deaf as those who will not hear.

- Time and tide wait for no man.

- Honesty is the best policy.

- A fool and his money are soon parted.

- Half a loaf is better than none.

- Every cloud has a silver lining.

- Out of sight, out of mind.

- When in Rome, do as the Romans do.

- A friend in need is a friend indeed.

- A watched pot never boils.

- He who laughs last laughs loudest.

- When the cats are away, the mice will play.
- A penny saved is a penny gained.
- There is none so blind as those that will not see.
- All that glitters is not gold.
- God helps those who help themselves.
- Beauty is in the beholder.
- A stitch in time saves nine.
- Where there is a will there is a way.
- Slow but sure wins the race.
- Never say die.
- Money doesn't grow on trees.
- Persuasion is better than force.
- Like father like son.
- Don't bite the hands that feed you.
- Beggars cannot be choosers.
- Actions speak louder than words.
- Practice makes perfect.
- All good things must come to an end.
- If you can't beat them join them.
- Two heads are better than one.
- Don't put all of your eggs in one basket.
- Better late than never.
- The grass is always greener on the other side.
- Do unto others what you would have them do unto you.

- All is well than ends well.
- Tit for tat.
- Diamonds cut diamonds.
- No pains no gains.
- Love begets love.
- No man can serve two masters.
- A drop in ocean.
- It's no use crying over spilled milk.
- Easy come easy go.
- Always put your best foot forward.
- You can't make an omelette without breaking a few eggs.
- If you scratch my back, I will scratch yours.
- Don't be afraid to change, you may lose something good but you may gain something better.
- If you wait for the perfect conditions, you will never set anything done.
- A joyful heart is good medicine.
- A close friend can become a close enemy.
- Follow your heart but take your brain with you.
- For every minute you are angry you lose sixty seconds of happiness.
- The best time to make friends is better when you need them.
- There is no elevator to success, you have to take the stairs.
- I have found that if you love life, life will love you back.

- I am a good enough person to forgive you but not enough to trust you again.
- A good life is when you smile, often dream big, laugh a lot and realize how blessed you are for what you have.
- Climb mountains not so the world can see you but you can see the world.
- Life is a one-time offer; use it well.
- You have become strong because of the pain you have faced and won.
- Never give up on something you can go a day without thinking about.
- Never reply when you are angry. Never make a promise when you are happy, never make a decision when you are sad.
- Being honest may not get you a lot of friends but it will always get you the right ones.
- Life is about sharing your happiness with the others.
- The most dangerous liars are those who think they are telling the truth.

CHINESE PROVERBS

- Who asks is a fool for five minutes but who does not ask remains a fool forever.
- It is better to light a candle than course the darkness.
- If you want no one to know, don't do it.
- If you always give you will always have.
- To succeed consult three old people.
- Before preparing to improve the world, first look around your own home there times.
- If you want happiness for a life time, help someone else.
- Those who do not read are not better than those who cannot.
- Love your neighbours but don't pull down the fence.
- Give a man a fish and you feed him a day, teach a man to fish and you feed him for a life time.
- If you want happiness for an hour, take a nap.
  If you want happiness for a day, go fishing.
  If you want happiness for a month, get married.
  If you want happiness for a year, inherit a fortune.
  If you want happiness for a lifetime, help someone else.
- A murderer may be forgiven, an affront never.
- One generation plants the trees, the other gets the shade.
- Man is the head of the family, the woman is the neck that turns it.

- Learning is a treasure that follows its owner everywhere.
- If you are planning for a year sow rice,

  If you are planning for a decade plant trees,

  If you are planning for a lifetime educate people.
- A gem is not polished without rubbing, nor a man perfected without trials.
- Your teacher can open the door but you must enter by yourself.
- A wise man makes his own decisions, an ignorant man follows the public opinion.
- Be not afraid of growing slowly; be afraid of standing still.
- To talk much and arrive nowhere is the same as climbing a tree to catch a fish.
- The best time to plant a tree was 20 years ago. The second best time is now.
- There are many paths to the top of the mountain but the view is always the same.
- To know the road ahead ask those coming back.
- A bird does not sing because it has an answer. It sings because it has a song.
- A man who chases two rabbits catches neither.
- Failing to plan is planning to fail.
- Only he who has travelled the road knows where the deep holes are.

- Pearls don't lie on the seashore. If you want one, you must dive for it.
- To understand your parents love you, you must raise your children yourself.
- If you wish to know the mind of a man, listen to his words.
- Beware of a dagger hidden in a smile.
- Teaching by example is better than teaching my preaching.
- Whoever is your teacher, even for a day, consider your father (to respect and care for) your whole life.

AFRICAN PROVERBS

- If you want to go fast, go alone; if you want to go far, go together.
- It takes a whole village to raise a child.
- The path is made by walking!
- Being happy is better than being king.
- When there is no enemy within, the enemies outside cannot hurt you.
- If you close your eyes to facts, you will learn through accidents.
- The sheep will spend its entire life fearing the wolf, only to be eaten by the shepherd.
- The fool speaks, the wise listens.
- A wise man never knows all; only fools know everything.
- Work is good, as long as you don't forget to hire.
- A lie has many variations, the truth has none.
- The speaker of truth has no friends.
- When elephants fight it is the grass which suffers.
- If you are not the part of the solution, you are part of the problem.
- Smooth seas do not make skillful sailors.
- One falsehood spoils a thousand truths.
- Not to know is bad; not to wish to know is worse.

- The word uttered cannot be taken back.
- If you offend, ask for pardon; if offended, forgive.
- Nobody tells all he knows.
- When an old man dies, a library burns to the ground.
- However long the night the dawn will break.
- Kindness is a language which the blind can see and hear.
- If you educate a man, you educate an individual; when you educate a woman you educate a generation.
- Quarrels end but words once spoken never die.
- A fire and pregnancy cannot be kept secret.
- Everything is formed by habit even prayer.

JAPANESE PROVERBS AND SAYINGS

- Vision without action is day dream; action without vision is nightmare.

- Fall seven times, stand up eight.

- To love is nothing, to be loved is something, but to love and to be loved is everything.

- A village without elders is a life without roots.

- Always find a reason to laugh. It may not add to your life years but it will surely add life to your years.

- Everyone makes mistakes; that is why there is an eraser on every pencil.

- It is better to write down something once; then read it ten times.

- Beginning is easy, continuing is hard.

- Wisdom and virtue are like the two wheels on a cart.

- When you are thirsty, it is too late to think about digging a well.

- A single arrow is easily broken, but not ten in a bundle.

- When the character of a man is not clear to you, look at his friends.

- Life is for one generation, a good name is forever.

- When someone is really hungry, then there is no such things as "bad food".

- If you make a mistake don't hesitate to correct it.

JEWISH PROVERBS

- Whoever does not try does not learn.

- Pride is the mask of one's own fault.

- Who find faithful friends, finds a treasure.

- A mother understands what a child does not say.

- Don't sell the sun to buy a candle.

ANCIENT GREEK PROVERBS AND QUOTATIONS

- The truth is not beauty, beauty is love.
- Wisdom is knowing the truth and telling it.
- Constant dripping will wear away a stone.
- The only true wisdom consists in knowing that you know nothing.
- Even from a foe a man may learn wisdom.
- A truth spoken before its time is dangerous.
- Fool me once, shame on you. Fool me twice, prepare to die.
- Eat beans for lunch and have no friends at the dinner table.
- Better a drop of wisdom than an ocean of gold.
- Thinking evil is much the same as doing it.
- You can't shake hands with a clenched fist.
- Pay attention to your enemies for they are the first to discover your mistakes.
- He who laughs not in the morning laughs soon at noon.
- He who becomes a sheep is eaten by the wolf.
- An open enemy is better than a false friend.
- Time is a doctor who heals all griefs.
- Day by day, what you choose, what you think, what you do is who you become.
- Know how to listen and you will profit even from those who talk badly.

- Courage is knowing what not to fear.

- We live, not as we wish to, but as we can.

- If Gods do evil, they are not Gods.

- Everything comes from earth and everything ends in earth.

MISCELLANEOUS PROVERBS FROM DIFFERENT COUNTRIES

- A shared joy is a double joy; a shared sorrow is half a sorrow. (Swedish proverb)
- Words should be witched, not counted. (Yiddish proverb)
- If you can't live longer, live deeper. (Italian proverb)
- After the game, the king and pawn go into the same box. (Italian proverb)
- The beard does not make the philosopher. (Italian proverb)
- Where love rights, the impossible may be attained. (Indian proverb)
- When you were born, you cried and the world rejoiced. Live your life in such a manner that when you die, the world cries and you rejoice. (Indian proverb)
- A man who uses force is afraid of reasoning. (Kenyan proverb)
- He who does not travel, does not know the value of men. (Moorish proverb)
- Measure a thousand times and cut once. (Turkish proverb)
- Even though you know a thousand things, ask the man who knows one. (Turkish proverb)
- The most beautiful fig may contain a word. (Zulu proverb)
- A fault confessed is half redressed. (Zulu proverb)

- A spoon does not know the taste of soup, nor a learned fool the taste of wisdom. (Welsh proverb)
- There's a bad potato in every sack. (Welsh proverb)
- Whoever gossips to you will gossip about you. (Spanish proverb)
- There is no shame in not knowing; the shame lies in not finding out. (Russian proverb)
- Success and rest don't sleep together. (Russian proverb)
- What you see in yourself is what you see in the world. (Afghan proverb)
- The stone which cannot be lifted should be kissed. (Arabic proverb)
- Write the bad things that are done to you in sand but write the good things that happen to you on a piece of marble. (Arabic proverb)
- Do good and throw it in the sea. (Arabic proverb)
- All weather is passing. (Norwegian proverb)
- He who fears death cannot enjoy life. (Spanish proverb)
- All time spent in anger is time lost being happy. (Mexican proverb)
- Pride is said to be the last vice the good man gets clear of. (American proverb)
- Empty barrels make the most noise. (Icelandic proverb)
- A cat in mittens won't catch mice. (Galic proverb)

- When spider webs unite, they can tie up a lion. (Ethiopian proverb)
- The devil always takes back his gifts. (Ukrainian proverb)
- You must be calm to fight a tiger. (Thai proverb)
- The secret to living well and longer is: eat halt, walk double, laugh triple and love without measure. (Tibetan proverb)
- Don't think there are no crocodiles just because the water is calm. (Malawian proverb)

OTHER PROVERBS

- A slipped tongue damages more than a slipped foot.

- He who climbs a good tree gets a push.

- Truthfulness draws one closer to death.

- Chameleon claims to be fast is good and to be slow is also good.

- One person does not make or takes decision for the community.

- A good name is worth mentioning.

TEN COMMANDMENTS OF THE NATIVE AMERICAN INDIANS

1. Treat the earth and all that dwells therein with respect.

2. Remain close to the Great Spirit.

3. Show great respect to your fellow beings.

4. Work together for the benefit of all mankind.

5. Give assistance and kindness wherever needed.

6. Do what you know to be right.

7. Look after the well-being of mind and body.

8. Delicate a share of your efforts to the greater good.

9. Be truthful and honest at all times.

10. Take full responsibility for your actions.

Section 3

Miscellaneous quotations

Quotations by anonymous people

In this section of the book the author has included some important quotations by anonymous people that definitely need to be included in this book as they offer major life lessons.

- Don't mock people who seek your help; the sun which melts butter is the same sun that hardens clay.
- If you are not willing to learn, no one can help you. If you are determined to learn, no one can stop you.
- Your life isn't yours if you always care what others think.
- Nothing will bring you greater peace than minding your own business.
- Smile at people who hate you!
- Never forget who helped you out while everyone else was making excuses.
- If you are right, no one remembers. If you are wrong, no one forgets.
- Our parents were patient when we were young, now it's our time to be patient during their old age.
- Knowledge without wisdom is possible but wisdom without knowledge is impossible.
- Two things prevent us from happiness: living in the past and observing others.
- Don't waste your time looking back on what you've lost. Move on. For life is not meant to be traveled backwards.

- Make sure everybody in your "boat" is rowing and not drilling holes.

- When you're not looking, know your circle.

- Inheritance is what you leave with people.
  Legacy is what you leave in them.

- A smile is a curve that sets everything straight.

- Pay attention to actions and never to words.

- Actions show; words deceive.

- I am not impressed by money, status or job title.
  I am impressed by the way you treat other human beings.

- Lotus is only the flower that teaches us where we reach is important; not where we came from.

- When we sleep on flowers, it's called our first night.
  But if flowers sleep on us, it's called our last night.
  And that is the reality of life!

- I never saw God, but I saw his greatness.

- You meet people who forget you, you forget people you meet, but sometimes you meet those people you can't forget. Those are your real friends.

- Leadership is a leader who knows the way, goes and shows the way.

- Never see what has been done.
  Only see what remains to be done.

- Before you judge me, make sure you are perfect.

If you are not then shut up.

- Live life to express; not to impress.
- Train your mind to be calm in every situation.
- Do everything with a good heart and expect nothing in return; and you will never be disappointed.
- Calling someone ugly will not make you pretty; do not criticize God's creations.
- Oh God, don't let me be away from you, even for a blink of an eye.
- Never say mean words out of anger.
  Your anger will pass, but your mean words can scare a person for life, so use kind words or be silent.
- Life is not about being rich, popular, highly educated or being perfect. Life is about being really humble and kind.
- A wise man once told his wife nothing because he was wise.
- Do good with intention; not for attention.
- You can see people's sins but not their repentance.
- Dear God,
  If I hurt others give me strength to apologize…
  If others hurt me give me strength to forgive.
- The worst feeling isn't loneliness...
  It's being forgotten.
- Fake people gossip about everyone else.
  Real people mind their own business.

- The biggest wall you've got to climb is the one you build in your mind.
- Silence isn't empty; it's full of answers.
- If they respect you, respect them;
    If they disrespect you, respect them.
- Do not lower your integrity for anyone.
- Real man does not love many girls;
    he loves the same girl in many ways.
- I take time to listen because I know exactly how it feels to be heard.
- Don't judge my choices when you understand my reasons.
- People start hating you when they can't reach your level.
- I may not be perfect. But I'm not fake and I'm proud of it.
- Mother is the blessing that no one can replace.
- There's someone out there envying the little things you fail to appreciate!
- Don't be afraid of losing people, be afraid of losing yourself by trying to please everyone.
- Keep your distance from people who will never admit they are wrong and always try to make you feel like it's all your fault.
- A bad attitude is like a flat tire; you can't go anywhere until you change it.
    It's not how big the house is. It's how happy the home is.

- Ego is not important in life but self-respect is the most important in life.
- Next time when you think of beautiful things, don't forget to count yourself in.
- A woman's loyalty is tested when her man has nothing.
  A man's loyalty is tested when he has everything.
- Those who put their trust will never be disappointed.
- Be so busy that you have no time to be sad.
- People ask you what you do for a living, so that they can calculate the level of respect to give you.
- Health is not just about what you're eating;
  it is also about what you're thinking, saying and believing.
- Having knowledge means nothing but using it means everything.
- It's nice to be important, but it's also important to be nice.
- Build your character in such a way, that even in a dark room, a girl can feel safe with you.
- Don't lose hope; you never know what tomorrow will bring.
- Don't worry about getting old, worry about thinking old.
- You are free to choose, but you are not free from the consequence of your choice.
- Patience is not the ability to wait, but the ability to keep a good attitude while waiting.
- Don't waste your life trying to impress others.

- Everything will be fine. It is just a matter of time.
- The biggest asset in the world is your mindset!
- Children do not judge you, they note what you do.
- If you want to know someone's mind, listen to their words.
  If you want to know someone's heart, watch their actions.
- Spiritual maturity is when you stop trying to change others...
  Instead focus on changing yourself.
- Everyone you meet is fighting a battle you know nothing about.
  Be kind always.
- No one stays with you permanently so, learn to survive alone.
- Life begins where fear ends.
- It's not about who is real in your face.
  It's about who stays loyal behind your back.
- Nothing in the world can trouble you as much as your own thoughts.
- Never let the sadness of your past, and the fear of your future, ruin the happiness of your present.
- Behind every good kid is a mom.
- Failure is not the opposite of success. It is part of success.
- Never judge someone by the opinion of others.
- Be like a diamond; precious and rare; not like a stone found everywhere.

- A mother is your first friend, your best friend. Your forever friend.

- Talk about your blessings more then you talk about your problems.

- Happiness is not about getting all you want; it is about enjoying all you have.

- A happy person is happy, not because everything is right in his life.
  He is happy because his attitude towards everything in his life is right.

- A boy who bought his own Toyota is more successful than the boy who shows off his dad's Lamborghini.

- Your speed doesn't matter, forward is forward.

- Character is how you treat those who can do nothing for you.

- Doubt everything is the world but never doubt yourself and your capabilities.

- Never stop praying! Prayer can change everything!

- Things change, people change, but God remains the same forever!

- Use your smile to change the world; don't let the world change your smile.

- Never hurt your mother; nothing is more painful than seeing tears in her eyes.

- You cannot wake a person who is pretending to be asleep.

- Quran is the best cure for the soul.

- Never get tired of praying because God is always listening.

- Intelligence without ambition is a bird without wings.

- Egoism is contagious.

- Only a hungry man can understand the pain of hunger.

- In the war of ego, the loser always wins.

- Know your worth; because people will try to give you less than you deserve.

- If someone tells you "You can't", they're showing you their limits; not yours!

- A successful day starts with fair and Quran.

- Everything is "pre-written" but with prayers it can be "re-written".

- If you don't know the whole story shut up.

- Making too many mistakes is fine, but making the same mistake too many times is not.

- Fear has two meanings; forget everything and run or face everything and rise.

- First question when I reach home is, "where is mom?"
  Even though I don't need her when I see her, I feel better.

- Love is when the other person's happiness is more important than your own.

- A family does not need to be perfect.
  It just needs to be united.

- Having a sharp memory is a good quality of the brain; but the ability to target unwanted things is a far better quality of the heart.
- Worries and tensions are like birds;

    We cannot stop them from being near us.

But we can certainly stop them from making a nest in our mind.

- A calm mind is the ultimate weapon against any challenge in life.
- Create your identity in such a way where, if superstitions enter, the brain is gone.
- When you help others, God will help to you in return.
- Always listen to people when they are angry.

    That is when the truth comes out.

- Never post your achievements. Post stupid stuff and jokes; so they will think you have no future; people hate progress. Seriously!
- Being a good person does not get you loved, it gets you wiser.
- Life and time are the world's best teachers;

    Life teaches us to make good use of time;

    and time teaches us the value of life.

- Sometimes you have to keep your good news to yourself. Everybody is not genuinely happy for you.
- Anger is the feeling that makes your mouth work faster than your mind.
- She: Leave my hand; we're in public.

He: Let the world know that you are my world.

- I may not be where I need to be.

  But I thank God I am not where I used to be!

- Your life becomes a masterpiece when you learn to master peace.

- If someone doesn't appreciate your presence, let them appreciate your absence.

- One of the most sincere forms of respect is actually to listen to what another has to say.

- If you want to live a life you've never lived, you have to do things you've never done.

- Strong people don't put others down; they lift them up.

- Givers have to learn to set limits because they don't have any.

- We need a leader not in love with money but in love with justice.

- When you're up in life, your friends get to know who you are.

  When you are down in life, you get to know who your friends are.

- One step is a testing; the next step is a blessing.

- Never underestimate how far a jealous person will go to destroy you.

- Some people are so poor but so rich by heart.

- Never forget who was with you when no one else was.

- Instead of worrying about what you cannot, shift your energy to what you can create.
- The past is your head, the future is your hands.

   You will never understand until it happens to you.

   Ability is what you are can capable of doing.

   Motivation determines what you do.

   Attitude determines how will you do it.
- A mistake that makes you humble is better than an achievement that makes you arrogant.
- Accept the fact that you cannot control everything; the only thing you can control 100% of the time is your attitude.
- The most beautiful eyes are those that seek beauty in others.
- Never wait for the perfect moment; just take a moment and make it a perfect.
- The truth is the truth, even if no one believes it.

   A lie is a lie, even if everyone believes it.
- Don't worry, don't be afraid ever because this is just a ride.
- The ones who are crazy enough to think they can change the world are the ones who do.
- You never know how close you are; never give up on your dreams.
- The real measure of your wealth is how much you would be worth if you lost all your money.
- We may have different religions, different languages, differently colored skin, but we all belong to one human race.

- When apples are four and we are five, my mother says "I don't like apples".
- Trust is like glass, once broken it will never be the same again.
- When you are in a position to help someone, do it gladly because it might be God answering someone's prayer through you.
- No one can do everything, but everyone can do something.
- No one is perfect! That's the reason why pencils have erasers.
- A true leader doesn't create separation.

  A true leader brings people together.

- A woman cannot change a man because she loves him; a man can change himself because he loves her.
- When the elderly die a library is lost and volumes of wisdom and knowledge are gone.
- A smile can mean a thousand words, but it can also hide a thousand problems.
- Jealousy comes in jokes, just pay attention.
- Sometimes you have to leave not for ego but for self-respect.
- Elegance is not about being noticed;
  It's about being remembered.
- People say a lot so I watch what they do.
- True love requires faith, trust and loyalty, not chocolate, flowers and expensive gifts.

- When you die people cry and beg for you to come back, but when you're here they don't even show they care about you.
- It's not what you look at that matters.
  It's what you see.
- You will never be good enough for everyone; but you will always be good for someone who really appreciates you.
- Don't feel bad if someone rejects you; people reject expensive things because can't afford them.
- However good or bad a situation, it will change.
- Sometimes the eyes can say more than the mouth.
- When men are oppressed, it's tragedy.
  When women are oppressed, it's tradition.
- Ambition with no determination has no destination.
- Laughter is the best medicine.
  But if you laugh for no reason, you need medicine.
- Jealousy is the last class to attend before becoming a witch.
- Always hope but never expect because expectations always hurt!
- Ego is just a small three-letter word, which can destroy a big twelve-letter word called "RELATIONSHIP".
- The sweetest time of the day is when you pray.
  Because you are talking to the one who loves you the most.
- Help the needy, the generous!
- Be a giver not a "taker".

- What other people think of you is none of your business.
- Times heals everything.
- Respect is the foundation of any relationship.
- When you see something beautiful or good in someone, tell them; it may take seconds to say, but for them, it could cost a lifetime.
- Self-respect is everything.
- Wife is cute when she is mute; and husband is honey when he gives money.
- Go for someone who is proud to have you.
- Keep your parents with you; they will give social, emotional, moral and psychological support to their grandchildren. Your money and status cannot buy it.
- Real richness is when you are so expensive, that no one can buy your character.
- Fake people have an image to maintain; real people just don't care.
- If you can stay positive in a negative situation, you win.
- The worst distance between two people is misunderstanding.
- Eat breakfast like a king, lunch like a prince and dinner like a pauper.
- Life isn't fair but, it's still good.
- You don't have to win every argument; agree to disagree.
- No one is in charge of your happiness except you.

- Don't tell people your plans, show people your results.
- Don't worry what people say behind your back, because God is going to bless you in front of their faces.
- When people put you down, God always picks you up.
- Discussion is always better than arguments. Because an argument is to find out who is right; and a discussion is to find what is right.
- Successful people build each other up, inspire and push each other. They motivate. Unsuccessful people just hate, blame and complain.
- Feed a dog for three days; it will remember you for three years. Feed a human for three years; they will forget you in three days.
- A great relationship is about two things: first, appreciating the similarities and second, respecting the differences.
- Fight all your battle with prayer. You will always win.
- An open enemy is better than a false friend.
- A clear rejection is always better than fake promises.
- I could be 18 or 81; my mom would still ask me where I'm going.
- Always love your mother because you will never get another.

- Always give without remembering and always receive without forgetting.
- Love does not die because of distance; it dies because of doubt.
- Saying is nothing.
  Doing is everything.
- A good husband is not a man who is rich or handsome, he is a man who knows the value of a woman.
- Better to become a second wife of any successful person than first wife of a stupid person.
- Never trust words; some people have sugar on their lips but venom in their hearts.
- The best thing about the worst time of your life is that you get to see the true colours of everyone.
- It's always better to be unique than the best; because being the best makes you the number one; but being unique makes you the only one.
- It takes around two years to learn to speak, but it takes a life time to learn what not to speak.
- Beauty catches the attention but character catches the heart.
- Someone just told me "loyal women stay home". Naah!
  Loyal women stay loyal no matter where they go.
- Be patient.
  Sometimes you have to go through the worst to get to the best.

- Love is like war; easy to start, hard to end and impossible to forget.
- Value the person who gives you time.

  It's not time; they share a part of life with you.
- Right person, wrong time.

  Right time, wrong person.

  New person, old lies.

  Old person, new lies.
- One of the best feelings in the world is knowing that someone is happy because of you.
- Confidence is better than perfection.

  Because perfection means doing the best but confidence means knowing how to handle the worst.
- Kindness makes you the most beautiful person in the world no matter what you look like.
- Life is beautiful.
- One day, one hour and even one minute will not come again.
- Avoid fights and anger and speak kindly to everyone you meet.
- The biggest advantage of walking on the path of honesty is that there is no crowd.
- Don't expect to get what you give.

  Not everyone has a heart like yours.
- A real woman doesn't love a million men.

  She loves one man in million ways.

- Until you spread your wings, you will have no idea how far you can fly.
- Sometimes it's better to just remain silent and smile.
- Your kiss is my drug;
  Your hug is my heaven;
  Your love is my life.
- I am responsible for what I say;
  I am not responsible for what you understand.
- God is like oxygen; you cannot see him but you cannot live without him.
- My heart is made to love you;
  My lips are made to kiss you;
  My eyes are made to see you.
- A mistake is something that happens accidently.
  Cheating and lying are not accidents; they are choices.
- Sometimes you have to lose a little to a gain a lot.
- There are many people who know you; but there are few who understand you.
- You'll never live a happy life if you're always worried about what others think of you.
- You can do 99 things for some people and all they remember is the one thing you didn't do.
- The most dangerous liars are those who think they are telling the truth.

- One loyal friend is worth a thousand relatives.
- Sometimes you have to make a decision that will break your heart but will give peace to your soul.
- Don't trust anyone, life is full of fake people.
- No love in this world is greater than a mother's love.
- The secret to happiness is low expectations.
- Love is not finding someone to live with, it is finding someone you can't live without.
- Don't go beyond your limits;
  But be perfect in your limits.
- To feel good is to look good.
- Never explain; your friends do not need it and your enemies will not believe it.
- Everything happens for a reason.
- Forgiveness is not something we do for other people;
  we do it for ourselves to get well and move on.
- Letting go is hard but sometimes holding on is harder.
- Walking with a friend in the dark is better than walking alone in the light.
- A good friend is hard to find, harder to leave and impossible to forget.
- If your relationship does not make you a better person, then you are with the wrong person.
- You don't need someone to complete you.

You only need someone to accept you completely.

- We enter the world alone, we leave the world alone.

  So, it's better to be alone.

- Some hearts understand each other even in silence.

- No one is you and that is your power.

- The most beautiful thing about you is your heart.

- True love stories never have endings.

- You are ripped at every edge.

  But you are a master piece!

- It is not too late to love yourself again.

- Why it is so easy to kill our happiness

  but so hard to kill our sadness?

- We ignore truth for temporary happiness.

- The eyes are useless when the mind is blind.

- I fall in love with souls; not faces.

- Your heart will never lie to you; that's the brain's job.

- I hope you find someone who knows how to love you when
  you are sad.

- It is not what we have in life,

  but who we have in our life that matters.

- Characterize people by their actions, and you will never be
  fooled by their words.

- It is better to be hated for what you are, than to be loved for
  something you are not.

- In life, there are difficult choices you must make.

  Let in and let go.

- Love is like dark chocolate;

  however dark it may be,

  you still want it because it is chocolate.

- Here is a piece of advice:

  Never put your happiness in someone else's hands.

- Love is like the wind; you can't see it but you can feel it.

- Don't chose the one who is beautiful; choose the one who

  makes your world beautiful.

- Beautiful things aren't always good but good things are

  always beautiful.

- The greatest distance on earth is not north and south, it is

  when I am right in front of you and you do not know that I

  love you.

- We fall in love by chance;

  we stay in love by choice.

- Distance never separates two hearts that really care.

- Good humor is the health of the soul, and sadness is its

  poison.

- Truth will ultimately prevail where there is pains to bring it

  to light.

- Worry is the interest paid by those who borrow trouble.

- My feeling is that there is nothing in life but refraining from hurting others and comforting those who are sad.
- When I cry about one thing I end up crying about everything that was wrong.
- Being with someone who does not love you is not called loyalty; it is called stupidity.
- The saddest thing is when you are feeling really down, you look around and realize that there is no shoulder for you.
- Respect yourself enough to walk away from anything that no longer serves you, grows you and makes you happy.
- Smile, even if it's a sad smile.
  Because sadder than a sad smile is the sadness of not knowing how to smile.
- Never apologize to others for their misunderstanding of who you are!
- Smile and silence are two powerful tools.
  Smile is the way to solve many problems.
  Silence is the way to avoid many problems.
- Do what 99% is not doing.
- The key to success is hard work and determination.
- Enjoy life today, yesterday is gone and tomorrow may never come.
- You can't start the next chapter of your life, if you keep re-reading the last one.

- You can't keep hurting a person and expect them to keep loving you.
- Silence is the best response to a fool.
- Never lie to someone who trusts you and never trust someone who lies to you.
- One woman can make a difference but together we can rock the world.
- Be a girl with a mind, a woman with attitude, and a lady with class.
- Don't be a woman that needs a man. Be a woman a man needs.
- Never stop learning because life never stops teaching.
- Start where you are; use what you have.
- Sometimes it is better to be alone. Nobody can hurt you.
- A useless life is an early death.
- Sadness is the result of unhappy thoughts.
- I did everything right for someone that does everything wrong.
- It is hard to forget someone who gave you so much to remember.
- When your absence doesn't change someone's life, then accept the reality that our presence has no meaning in their life.
- All birds find shelter during rain but eagles avoid rain by flying above the clouds.
- Aim for the moon; if you miss, you may hit a star.
- Don't watch the clock: do what it does; keep going.

- Wrong is wrong even if everyone is doing it.
  Right is right even if nobody is doing it.
- The problem isn't a problem; the problem is your attitude about the problem.
- If you don't want anyone to find out don't do it.
- Hugging is a silent way of saying you matter to me.
- Sometimes all you need is a hug from the right person and all the stress just melts away.
- Life is like a coin:
  Pleasure and pain are two sides; only one side is visible at a time.
  But remember the other side is waiting for its turn.
- Anyone who can think is a philosopher.
- Expectation is not greed.
- The easiest way to be unique is to be yourself.
- Cleanliness is next to the Godliness.
- The richer we become materially, the poorer we become morally and spiritually.
- I am a simple person with a complicated mind.
- Society is funny; they ask you to be yourself and yet they judge you.
- Sometimes, those with so much to say are silent.
- Work hard in silence; let success make all the noise.
  Silence is the most powerful scream.

- Life always offers you a second chance. It's called tomorrow.
- When life gives you a hundred reasons to show life that you have a thousand reasons to smile.
- Behind every successful man there's a lot of unsuccessful years.
- I never dreamed about success. I worked for it.
- A goal without a plan is just a wish.
- Success does not come to you, you go to it.
- Be thankful for the hard times for they have made you.
- If you really want to do something you will find a way; if you don't, you will find an excuse.
- Never give up; believe in yourself.
- Nothing will change unless you change yourself.
- Sometimes later becomes never.
- Every story has an end, but in life every end is a new beginning.
- Stop comparing yourself to other people; you're supposed to be unique.
- Be a better version of yourself.
- Do not let yourself be controlled by three things: People, money or past experiences.
- Do not compare yourself with anyone else in this world. If you do, you are insulting yourself.

- Nobody can make you happy until you're happy with yourself first.
- This world is full of monsters with friendly faces.
- Nothing is permanent!
  Don't stress yourself too much because no matter how bad the situation, it will change.
- The happiest people don't have the best of everything. They make the best of everything.
- Silence will always be the best revenge; and love will always be all you need.
- Act like a king to be respected like a king.
- Smile because it is easier than explaining what is wrong.
- Smile will always be the best medicine.
- You are not fully dressed without a smile.
- Always remember to be happy because you never know who is falling in love with your smile.
- Smile and forgive. It is the only way to live.
- Do not cry for a man who's left you:
  The next one may fall for you smile.
- A warm smile is the universal language of kindness.
- Smile; it is the key that fits the lock of everybody's heart.
- Worry is a total waste of time; it doesn't change anything.
- Confidence and hard work is the best medicine to kill the disease called failure.

- Don't be afraid to change; you may lose something good, but you may gain something better.
- Overthinking is the biggest cause of unhappiness.
- Never get too attached to someone, because attachments lead to expectations and expectations lead to suffering.
- Your greatness is not what you have; it's what you give.
- A woman treats you how she wants to be treated first; then she treats you how you treat her.
- Self-clarification is an indication of weakness of one's intelligence.
- It hurts when the people who made you feel so special yesterday make you feel so unwanted today.
- Beautiful faces are everywhere but beautiful minds are hard to find.
- A gardener may water a plant daily but fruits grow only in the season.
- Have patience; everything is destined to happen at its own time.
- The strongest people make time to help others, even if they are struggling with their own problems.
- Life is the most difficult exam.
- Many people fail because they try to copy others, not realizing that everyone has a different question paper.
- Being different makes you beautiful.

- Trust is like a sticker; once it is removed it may stick again but will not be as strong as it holds when you first applied it.
- I don't trust words, I trust actions. People can tell you anything, but actions tell you everything.
- You trust a rabbit; the tortoise only wins in the book; real life races are very different.
- Whatever is taken away from you will be replaced with something better.
- If you are not doing what you love, you are wasting your time.
- There is no wealth like knowledge and no poverty like ignorance.
- People say, "Find good people and leave the bad ones". But I say, "find the good in people and ignore the bad in them". Because "no one is perfect".
- Your parents didn't leave you when you were young, so don't leave them when they are old.
- There is nothing more beautiful than someone who goes out of their way to make life beautiful for others.
- Kindness is limitless.
- They told me not to play with fire or I would be burned. I told them you can't get burned when you are the flame.
- Silence is the best answer to someone who doesn't value your word.

- One beautiful heart is more important than a million beautiful faces.
- A beautiful life doesn't just happen. It is built daily by prayers, humility, sacrifice and love.
- Don't do things to be noticed or praised. Do things simply because they are the right things to do.
- What you want will not happen; what you need will definitely happen.
- Relationships end because girls love too much and boys love too many.
- Every moment we spend worrying about tomorrow is a moment we lost enjoying today.
- By the time you realize that your father was right, you will have a son who thinks that you are wrong.
- If you depend on Allah (God) you're already winning.
- The most difficult phase of life is not when no one understands you; it is when you don't understand yourself.
- Nothing is heavier on the believer scale on the day of judgement than a good character.
- Your self-worth is determined by you, you don't have to depend on someone telling you who you are.
- We are the generation who listens to their parents and also the first which has to listen their children. We are not exactly special: we are limited edition.

- You cannot talk butterfly language with caterpillar people.
- Education and money put you on a balanced life.
  A life without education and money leaves you in the dark.
- Knowledge is knowing what to say.
  Wisdom is knowing when to say it.
  Humility is being honest about your weaknesses.
- Behind every successful man there is a woman and behind a happy woman there is a loyal man.
- Memories are always special. Sometimes we laugh by recalling the days we cried and sometimes we cry while recalling the days we laughed.
- If you want a long relationship, follow one simple rule; never lie.
- Be careful what you tell people; a friend today could be an enemy tomorrow.
- Be valuable; not available.
- There is no reason to work back when you have so much to look forward to.
- People respect you or not but always do your good work, because the sun is rising even when millions of people are sleeping.
- We spend money we don't have on things we don't need to impress people who don't care.
- Remember when you point a finger at someone. There is one more pointing back at you.

- If you don't clear your misunderstanding in time, it becomes the reasons for distance forever.
- Beautiful girls are mostly single because no one believes they are single.
- I want to be with you for only two times; now and forever.
- Prayer doesn't have to be perfect; it must be sincere.
- The best outfit is self-respect; don't lose it.
- Your child's behavior and attitude will depend on how you raise him/her.
- If you want to be remembered after you die, borrow money everyone you know.
- Life is an echo.

  What you send out comes back.

  What you saw you reap.

  What you give you get.

  What you see in others exists in you.
- Don't judge so you will not be judged.
- Radiate and give love and love will come back to you.
- Don't blame people for disappointing you; blame yourself for expecting too much from them.
- Being single is so difficult, you fall in love with every other person you see.
- If we judge people nobody is yours.

  If we understand people, everybody is yours.

- Develop the habit of understanding and you will experience peace, love in all relations.
- Sometimes God breaks your heart to save your soul.
- Sometimes in life we just need a hug. No words, no advice, just a hug to make you feel better.
- A dog is the only animal on earth that loves you more than he loves himself.
- Work for a cause; not for applause.
- Perfection is not attainable, but if we chase perfection, we can catch excellence.
- If you are searching for that one person who will change your life look into the mirror.
- Love doesn't need to be perfect; it just needs to be true.
- Affection is more important than perfection.
- Accept the fact that some people will never like you.
- It is hard to fly when something is weighting you down.
- Go after dreams; not people.
- Life and time are the world's best teachers. Life teaches us the use of time and time teaches us the value of life.
- The sign of a beautiful person is that they always see beauty in others.
- Man says, "when money will come, I will do something". Money says, "do something; then I will come".

- Some people love you but don't tell you, some people tell you but don't love you.
- I learn to give not because I have much, but because I know exactly how it feels to have nothing.
- A good book can change your life.
- Bad times are the best time to know who really cares.
- No book, no life.
  Know book, know life.
- No response is a response and it is a powerful one; remember that.
- A woman who doesn't ask for anything, deserves everything.
- Never forget the hands that raised you.
- Remember when forgiving you heal, and when you let go you grow.
- Happy people focus on what they have.
- Burn your ego before it burns you.
  - Life is a combination of adjustments and compromises. Adjust when someone wants to be with you and compromise when you want to be with someone.
  - Don't be so quick to believe what you hear, because lies spread faster than the truth.
  - Never lose hope; God is never late to do miracles for you.
  - No matter how far you are, I will wait for you until we

can finally be together.

- Those who leave everything in God's hands will eventually see God's hands in everything.
- If people are trying to bring you down it only means that you are above them.
- The most important thing in the world is family and love.
- God doesn't give us what we can handle; God helps us handle what we are given.
- Easy is to judge the mistake of others, difficult is to realize your own mistakes.
- When I was a kid, I used to admire educated people, but now I realized well-mannered people are better than well-educated ones.
- If you want to lose weight, don't diet or exercise; just fall in love with the wrong guy.
- Oh God, grant me a mind free of worry, a heart free of sadness and a body free of sickness.
- A best gift a man can give his woman is time, respect and his attention.
- Keep going; everything will come to you at the perfect time.
- Love is like the rain, we never know when it comes and how long it will last.
- Knowledge is a tool and wisdom is the craft in which the tool is used.

- Kindness makes you the most beautiful person in the world no matter what you look like.
- Don't forget to give a smile to your haters every time you face them.
- Choose a good heart; not a good face.
- It is not what we have in life, but who we have in life that matters.
- 80% of women use silence to express pain.
- Sometimes you have to leave not for ego but for self-respect.
- The happiest people in life are the givers; not the receivers.
- Until my last breath I will give thanks to the lord.
- If you keep your pride, your ego and your self-significance down, you will become available to grace.
- Work hard, stay disciplined and be patient. Your time will come.
- A lot of problems in the world would disappear if we talked to each other instead of talking about each other.
- Our prime purpose in this life is to help others. And if you can't help them, don't hurt them.
- Faith is taking the first step even when you don't see the whole staircase.
- No matter how many times the teeth bite the tongue, they still stay and work together. That is the spirit of forgiveness and relationship.

- Understand that you owe nothing. Everything surrounding you is temporary; only the love in your heart will last forever.

- People will come and go in life. But the person in the mirror will be there forever. So, be good to yourself.

- If you light a lamp for someone else it will also brighten your path.

- When you move your focus from competition to contribution life becomes a contribution. Never try to defeat people, just win their hearts.

- Never regret being a good person to wrong people.

- Your behavior says everything about you and their behavior says enough about them.

- No one in this world is pure and perfect. If you avoid people for their little mistakes you will always be alone. So, judge less and love more.

- Never stop learning because life never stops teaching.

- Making a hundred friends is not a miracle. The miracle is to make a single friend who will stand by your side even when hundreds are against you.

- If a drop of water falls in a lake there is no identity but if it falls on a leaf it shines. So, choose the best place where your ability shines.

- Our destiny is not created by the shoes we wear but by the steps we take.

- Nobody is superior, nobody is inferior, but nobody is equal either. People are simply unique. Incomparable.
  You are you; I am I..

- The best preparation for tomorrow is doing your best today.

- God is the best listener; you don't have to shout nor cry loud because he hears even the silent prayer of a sincere heart.

- All stress, anxiety, depression, is caused when we ignore who we are and start living to please others.

- When we are wrong and we surrender, it means we are honest.
  When we are right and surrender, it means we value relations.

- Life is the most difficult exam. Many people fall because they try to copy others, not realizing that everyone has a different question paper.

- Respect is like a mirror. The more you show it to other people, the more it will reflect back on you.

- Love what you have, need what you want, accept what you receive.

- Give what you can; always remember what goes round, comes around!

- A pretty face gets old. A nice body will change but a good heart will always be good.
- Running away from any problem will only increase the distance from the solution. Face it and finish it.
- Relationships are not exams to pass or fail and not a competition to win or lose, but it's a feeling in which you care for someone more than yourself.
- The strongest factor for success is self-esteem; believing you can do it; believing you deserve it; believing you will get it.
- Forget who hurt you yesterday, but don't forget those who love you every day.

  Forget the past that makes you cry and focus on the present that makes you smile.

  Forget the pain, but never the lessons you gained.
- When you look for the good in others, you discover the best in yourself.
- If you have to choose between being kind and being right, choose being kind and you will always be right.
- All we have to decide is what to do with the time that is given to us.
- The best view comes after the hardest climb.
- If you want to fly, you have to give up the things that weigh you down.

- Our destiny is not written for us; it's written by us.
- Everything you want is on the other side of fear.
- Your past mistakes are meant to guide you; not to define you.
- The days are long, but the years are short.
- You cannot go back and change the beginning, but you can start where you are and change the ending.
- You cannot change how people feel about you.
- Most of your sins are because of your tongue.
- Beware of jealousy, for it destroys your character just as fire destroys wood.
- Speak the truth even if it's bitter.
- Trust Allah (God) but tie your camel.
- Lucky is the woman whose first child is a daughter.
- Speak a good word or remain silent.
- Feed the hungry, visit the sick, set free the captives.
- A nation's strength ultimately consists in what it can do on its own and not in what it can borrow from others.
- Once a wise man was asked "what is meaning of life?" He replied, "life itself has no meaning; life is an opportunity to create a meaning."
- Simplicity is the jewel of life.
- When you help others, God will help you in return.
- Always remember care should be in heart not in words,

anger shall be in words not in heart.

- Be kind.
- People tend to forget their debits but remember their rights.
- Disagree to agree.
- The power to question is the basic of all human progress.
- In childhood, we smile for no reason. In adulthood, we smile to hide the reason.
- The most beautiful thing you can wear is confidence.
- Smart people know what they want. Wise people know what they don't want.
- Be kind to unkind people; they need it the most.
- We all die; the goal isn't to leave forever, the goal is to create something that will last forever.
- A woman with a beautiful body is good for a night, but a woman with a beautiful mind is good for a lifetime.
- A flower does not think of competing with the flowers next to it; it just blooms.
- The greatest distance between two people is misunderstanding.
- The worst person to be around is someone who complains about everything and appreciates nothing.
- Talent takes you to the top but behaviour decides how long you stay there.
- Fear has two meanings:

Forget everything and run.

Face everything and rise... the choice is ours.

- Ego is the only requirement to destroy any relationship; be a bigger person. Skip the "E" and let it "Go".

- Stop being always available to people who are just there for you when it's convenient for them.

- I need you, Lord.

  I am nothing without you.

- A father said to his son: "Be careful where you walk". The son responded: "You be careful; I walk in your footsteps".

- Life is very complicated.... When you have standards, people call it attitude; when you are simple, people try to cheat you and when you cheat others, people call you smart.

- A woman's beautiful face attracts a flirter. A woman's beautiful heart attracts a lover. A woman's beautiful character attracts a man.

- With trust even silence is understood. Without trust every word is misunderstood.

- Trust is the soul of all relationships.

- Everything is not something, because there is nothing.

- The only people who deserve to be in your life are the ones who treat you with love, kindness and respect.

- The best feeling in the world is to see others smiling because of you.

- Earth makes everything possible.

Hope makes everything work.

Love makes everything beautiful.

- We come with nothing, we go with nothing, but one great thing we can achieve in our beautiful life is.... a little remembrance in someone's mind and a small place in someone's heart.

- Being a good person is very difficult. It's like being a goalkeeper. No matter how many goals you saved, the people remember only the goals you missed.

- People change, feelings fade. Promises are broken but memories stay forever.

- Never lose hope in any condition, because darkness of night always ends with light of the day. Anything is possible.

- A moment of patience in a moment of anger saves you a hundred moments of regret.

- Your competitors can copy your work, your style or your procedure. But none can copy your passion.

- If you hold it firmly, the world is yours......!

- Be passionate.

- An attitude of positive expectations is the mark of the superior personality.

- Be honest when in trouble and simple when in wealth. Be polite when in authority and be silent when in anger. This is called the life management.

- If an egg is broken by outside force, life ends. If it is broken by inside force, life begins.

- Great things always begin from the inside. Don't waste your life trying to impress.

- Do everything with a good heart and expect nothing is return, and you will never be disappointed.

- The secret of every successful relationship is transparency.

- Understanding is deeper than knowledge. There are many people who know you but there are very few who understand you.

- Beware of ego. It's a double-edged sword. The out edge cuts your popularity, while the inner edge cuts your purity.

- No beauty shines brighter than that of a good heart.

- Trust and truth are the two pillars of a strong relationship.

- If you don't trust a person, you won't say the truth and if you don't say the truth the person won't trust you.

- The most useful asset of a person is not a head full of knowledge but a heart full of love with ears open to listen and hands willing to help.

- Your promises don't make you a better person. Your commitment does!

- A long flower still blossoms for its purpose…Not looking around for admirers…Stay true to your purpose, admirers will find their way to you.

- Always take extra care of three things in life… Promise, friendship and relationship because they don't make noise, but when they break they create silence!

- Time and good friends are two things that become more valuable the older you get.

- The lotus is a symbol of purity with roots in the mud; the flower remains above the dirty water. Live a lotus life; be in the world, but unaffected by any negativity.

- Positive thinking isn't about expecting the best to happen every time but accepting that whatever happens is the best for this moment.

- Any person can make you realize how wonderful the world is! But only few will make you realize how wonderful you are in the world; care for those few!

- Ego and love are the branches of the same tree; the only difference is, love always wants to say sorry and ego always wants to hear sorry.

- Kindness is more than deeds.

- Whenever you are in the position to help someone, just do it and be glad, because God is answering someone's prayers through you. So don't think that anybody is using you but remember that you're useful.

- Never share your secrets with anyone; this can be self-destructive. Perhaps the most important advice in life.
- Life is similar to a boxing game; defeat is not declared when you fall down. It is only declared when you refuse to get up.
- Even kings and emperors with heaps of wealth and vast dominion cannot compare with any filled with the love of God.
- Let no man in the world live in delusion.
- Riches cannot be gathered without sin and evil means.
- Don't be foolish taking pride in your social status, class, color or religion. Treat the whole human race as one and equal.
- From the one light, the entire universe welled up. So, who is good, and who is bad?
- Two things bring happiness and success in life:
  The way you manage when you have nothing and
  the way you behave when you have everything.
- As long as we don't forgive people who have hurt us, they occupy a rent free space in our mind.
- What is success? It is when your photos are uploaded on Google instead of Facebook.
- If a drop of water falls on a lake, its identity is lost; if it falls on a lotus leaf, it shines like a pearl. Drop is the same; but the company matters.

- Never win people with arguments rather defeat them with your smile, because people who wish to argue with you, cannot bear your silence.
- Always keep hoping for good; keep a green tree in your heart; the singing birds will automatically come.
- Never tell your problems to anyone; 20% don't care and the other 80% are glad you have them.
- Sea is common for all, some take pearls, some take fishes, some come out with wet legs. World is common to all; what we get is what we are looking for.
- A child asked God: "if everything is already written in destiny, then why should I wish?" God smiled and said: "maybe on some pages I have written, "As you wish".
- Use soft words and hard arguments.
- Everyone is gifted but some people never open their package.
- Never fear shadow; that always means there is a light shining somewhere.
- Tears are words the heart can't express.
- For life is only life when blest with health.
- Betrayal does that betrays the betrayer.
- Life without liberty is like a body without a spirit.
- The greater the power the more dangerous the abuse.
- To the world you may be one person but to one person, you may be the world.

- Growing old is mandatory; growing up is optional.
- Be kind; every argument is someone's ignorance.
- The more arguments you win the less friends you will have.
- The ego wants quantity, but the soul wants quality.
- Knowledge will give you power but the character will give you respect.
- Never laugh at someone's situation because you just never know if some day you will find yourself in the very same position.
- Who are we as human beings if we ignore the suffering of others?
- A person is either your brother in faith or your equal in humanity.
- Be humble and never think that you are better than anyone else. For dust you are; for dust you are and unto dust you shall return.
- Most of the problems in life come because of two reasons; we act without thinking and we keep thinking without acting.
- When you get what you want, that's God's direction. When you don't get what you want, that is God's protection.
- Every mother is a doctor without a medical degree.
- Remember when you point a finger at someone, there are three more fingers pointing back to you.
- Always listen twice; first what is being said; then, who said it.

- Walk away from arguments that lead to nowhere. Walk away from people who deliberately put you down. Walk away from the habit of pleasing people who never see your worth.

- Never explain yourself to anyone because the person who likes you doesn't need it and the person who dislikes you won't believe it.

- When problems come into your life like a non-stop rain, always remember that God will always be your umbrella.

- No matter how old you get you always want your mother when you don't feel good.

- Women with higher IQs have a harder time finding a mate. Intelligent women would rather remain single than be with the wrong person.

- Some people get hurt by words, some by actions and some by silence but the biggest hurt is someone ignoring us when we value them a lot.

- Don't be impressed by: money, followers, degrees and titles. Be impressed by: generosity, integrity, humility and kindness.

- Words may lie but actions will always tell the truth.

- Beautiful people are not always good but good people are always beautiful. Search for a beautiful heart not necessarily a beautiful face.

- The hardest question to answer; describe yourself.

- If what's ahead scares you and what's behind hurts you, then look up.

- Beauty is not important but a beautiful heart is the most important.
- Punctuality is not about being in time; it's basically about respecting your own commitments.
- Trying now is better than crying later.
- If you are tired learn to rest; not to quit.
- Anything is not easy but everything is possible.
- God is the best doctor and prayer is the best medicine.
- Everything is easy when you are crazy; nothing is easy when you are lazy.
- Your degree is just a piece of paper; your education shows in your behavior.
- Listen to everyone, learn from everyone because nobody knows everything but everyone knows something.
- My father said there were two kinds of people in the world; givers and takers. The takers may eat better but givers sleep better.
- Kill tension before tension kills you.
  Reach your goal before your goal kicks you.
  Live life before life leaves you.
- Dear mom, sometimes I may get angry at you but seriously I can't live without you.
- Be careful with your words; once they are said they can only be forgiven; not forgotten.

- Friends raise your spirit; enemies raise your standard.
- Kids are the best humans.
- We do not remember days; we remember moments.
- Worst feeling in the world? Being lied to by the person you love.
- A friend who is there for you in your bad times is a friend for a life time.
- How sinful are those youth who speak gently with their friends while they shout out at their parents.
- Life is full of fake people; trust no one.
- A mother can take care of ten children but sometimes ten children can't take care of one mother.
- The best form of respect is self-respect, give it to yourself and other will see that you won't settle for anything else.
- There is a difference between being liked and being valued. A lot of people like you, not many value you. Be valued.
- Follow your heart but take your brain with you.
- People do not decide their futures, they decide their habits and their habits decide their future.
- Staying positive does not mean you have to be happy all the time; it means even on hard times you know that better ones are coming.
- Strong friendship doesn't need daily conversation.

- If you're helping someone and expecting something in return you are doing business, not kindness.

- You have to learn the rules of the game and then you have to plan better than anyone else.

- Relationship with a nice person is like a sugarcane. You break it; crush it; squeeze it; even beat it or grind it; still you will get only sweetness.

- I don't have time to hate anyone. I either love you or I don't care at all.

- One beautiful heart is better than 1000 beautiful faces.

- When God blesses you financially, raise your standard of giving; not your standard of living.

- Gratitude is the best attitude.

- Discussions are always better than arguments because an argument is to find out who is right and discussion is to find out what is right.

- The richest of the rich is one who is not a prisoner to greed.

- A person becomes 10 times more attractive not by their looks but by their acts of kindness, respect, honesty and by the loyalty they show.

- If you do right no one remembers. If you do wrong, no one forgets.

- I don't care if you don't like me; I was not born to impress you.

- A lion never loses sleep over the opinions of sheep.
- If I have you by my side, then I have everything.
- If you tell the truth you don't have to remember anything.
- Money is numbers and numbers never end, if it takes money to be happy, your search for happiness will never end.
- Slow progress is better than no progress; stay positive and don't give up.
- Every pain gives a lesson and every lesson changes a person.
- Staying quiet doesn't mean I have nothing to say; it means I don't think you are ready to hear my thoughts.
- If the path is beautiful first confirm where it leads but if the destination is beautiful don't bother how the path is.
- Ladies, please stop wasting your time looking for Mr. Right; just find me, Mr. Left, and that idiot to the right.
- Being humble is better than being humbled!
- Never say mean words out of anger; you anger will pass but your mean words can scare a person for life, so use kind words or be silent.
- When the mind falls in love, it is temporary; when the heart falls in love, it lasts a lifetime; when the soul falls in love, it is eternal.
- Don't feel bad if people remember you only when they need you; feel privileged that you are like a candle that comes to their mind when there is darkness.

- What is stress? It's the gap between our expectation and reality. The more the gap the more the stress, so expect nothing and accept everything.
- When days are dark, friends are few.
- Love is a journey that never ends.
- Four things we cannot recover in life;
  Words after they are said;
  Movements after they are done;
  Actions after they are done;
  Time after it's gone.
- Some people are wise, some people are otherwise.
- Friendship is impossible with a liar.
- Talent is a gift but character is a choice.
- Our life does not get better by chance; it gets better by change.
- Pray not until God hears you but until you listen to God.
- Modern slaves are not in chain but in debt.
- Sometimes the chains that prevent us from being free are more mental than physical.
- Don't trust everything you see; even salt looks like sugar.
- Love when you are ready; not when you are lonely.
- Beauty does not last forever but a beautiful personality does.
- In order to learn a little we have to study a lot.

- Don't treat people as bad as they are; treat them as good as you are.
- When the hand of God is on your life, nobody can stop you from being blessed.
- Cheating on a good person is like throwing away a diamond and picking up a rock.
- Fake people gossip about everyone else. Real people mind their own business.
- Honesty is a very expensive gift; don't expect it from cheap people.
- Your mother is the only person that carries you for 9 months in her belly, 3 years in her arms and forever in her heart.
- Maturity is in the mind; not in age.
- Today a reader; tomorrow a leader.
- Birth: Given by others,

  Name: given by others,

  Income: given by others.

  First and last bath will be given by others after death your property and belongings will be taken by others.

  Still I wonder why we have the unnecessary ego problems in life.
- Let us all simplify our life and love.

  Live with others peacefully.

  The happiest people in life are the givers; not the receivers.

- Serve your parents in the last part of their life, just like they served you in the first part of your life.

- There is no greatest religion than humanity.

- Honesty is the first chapter in the book of wisdom.

- Pulling someone down will never help you reach the top.

- Have you ever looked back at your past and realized it was God who kept you alive?

- More than machinery, we need humanity; more than cleverness, we need kindness and gentleness.

- If you aren't grateful for what you already have, what makes you think you would be happy with more?

- The hardest walk is walking alone but it is also the walk that makes you stronger.

- Empty pocket teaches you a million things in life but full pocket spoils you in a million ways.

- The distance between dreams and reality is called action.

- You don't need money or gold to be rich. All you need is God in your life.

- Karma has no menu; you get served what you deserve.

- Mistakes are like diseases; realization is the medicine for it.

- Life is not about what you couldn't do so far; it is about what you still can do.

- Prove yourself to yourself; not others.

- Not all advice from old people you should listen to.

Remember foolish people grow old too.

- Don't be a parrot in life, be an eagle. A parrot talks way too much but can't fly high but an eagle is silent and has the willpower to touch the sky.
- Distance yourself from people who i. use you, ii. lie to you, iii. put you down, iv. disrespect you.
- Valentine's day without a partner is okay but mothers' day without a mother is very painful.
- Truth of life is that if you do a million good things nobody will care but commit a single mistake and everyone will judge you.
- Mom, without you, I am nothing.
- If you want to hear the sound of the bird, don't buy a cage; plant a tree.
- Choose a good heart; not a good face.
- Look back and be grateful.
Look ahead and be hopeful.
  Look around and be helpful.
- Life is a balance between holding on and letting go.
- If plan A didn't work, don't worry; the alphabet has 25 more letters.
- Live the best for today because you don't know what is going to happen tomorrow.
- Never wait; life goes faster than you think.

- Mother is a blessing that no one can replace.
- I don't trust anyone who is nice to me but rude to the waiter because they would treat me the same way if I were in that position.
- Don't be so proud of your skin color; we all are the same when light goes off.
- People want to see you doing better but not better than them.
- Love is a seed; if you care, it grows.
- Never assume that loud is strong and quiet is weak.
- Be a good person in real life; not in social media.
- No one is more hated than he who speaks the truth.
- No matter how big is the hammer you use, you can't pound common sense into stupid people.
- We can learn even from our enemies.
- To be loved, be loveable.
- The bold adventurer succeeds the best.
- He who is not prepared today will be less so tomorrow.
- Man conquers the world by conquering himself.
- Knowing yourself is the beginning of all wisdom.
- Nobody can give you better advice than yourself.
- The nourishment of the body is the food while the nourishment of the soul is feeding others.
- Children must be taught how to think; not what to think.
- My silence doesn't mean I agree with you; it means your

level of stupidity rendered me speechless.

- A man with one watch knows what time it is; a man with two watches is never quite sure.
- Don't look where you fell but where you slipped.
- Nothing brings you peace but yourself.
- People may doubt what you say but they will believe what you do.
- Be nice to people on your way up because you will need them on your way down.
- Time you enjoyed wasting was not wasted.
- While seeking revenge dig two graves, one for you too.
- Happiness has one advantage over wealth. No one can borrow it.
- Everything happens for a reason.
- Forgiveness is not something we do for other people; we do it for ourselves to get well and move on.

Quotations by famous people

In this part of the book the author included important quotations by various famous people, from philosophers and religious leaders to poets and fashion designers.

- Most of the important things in the world have been accomplished by people who have kept on trying when there seemed to be no hope at all. (Dale Carmegel)

- It is not who is right but what is right that is important. (Thomas Huxley)

- Islam will win, with or without you. But without Islam you will be lost and you will lose. (Ahmad Dedat)

- When you understand everything you can forgive everything. (Leo Tolstoy)

- You can be everything in life but the important thing is to be a good person. (Shams Tabriz)

- If you want to make your dream come true the first thing you have to do is wake up. (J.M. Power)

- There are only two rules for being successful. One, figure out exactly what you want to do; two, do it. (Mario Cuomo)

- All men make mistakes. But only wise men learn from their mistakes. (Winston Churchill)

- Industry is the soul of business and the key stone of prosperity. (Charles Dickens)

- Never think that God's delays are God's denials. Hold on; Hold fast; Hold out; Patience is genius. (De Buffon)

- One beautiful heart is better than a thousand beautiful faces. (Kuldip Singh)

- Don't be afraid of dying, be afraid of living with nothing to die for. (Nazmul Islam)

- Without education, it is complete darkness and with education it is light. Education is a matter of life. (Quaid -E-Azam)

- The aim of a chained man is to chain others, while the aim of free man is to free others. (Vermont Howard)

- Don't look to others to create yourself. Look within to allow to who you are to naturally be unveiled in the world. (Valley Martin)

- How is it possible that the most intellectual creature to ever walk the planet is destroying its only home? (Jane Goodall)

- The hardest job kids face today is learning good manners without seeing any. (Fred Astaire)

- Never underestimate the power of prayer. One small prayer can change your life forever. (Ameen)

- Good friends are like stars. You don't always see them, but you know they are there. (Christy Evans)

- Read a thousand books and your words will flow like a river. (Lisa See)

- If you keep breaking others people's hearts, whatever religious duty you perform is of no use. (Shams Tabriz)

- Ten beggars can sleep on one rug, but two kings feel uncomfortable in one country. (Saadi)
- Don't break a bird's wings and tell it to fly. (Najwa Zeisian)
- Meaningful silence is better than meaningless words. (Python Gores)
- Kill the negativity in you before it destroys your peace of mind. (Lenin Shende)
- The beauty of a man is dignity. (Hazart Ali)
- We were all humans until:
  Religion separates us, politics divides us, wealth classifies us and race disconnect us. (Sufi sayings)
- When someone gives you their trust, they are saying, "I am safe with you." Don't break it. Appreciate it. (Dubinsky)
- Someone's sitting in the shade today because someone planted a tree a long time ago. (Warren Buffett)
- The starting point of all achievement is desire. (Napoleon Hill)
- Whoever conceals the fault of Muslim, Allah (God) will conceal (his fault) on the day of resurrection. (Sahih-al-Bukhari (2442)
- Do not pay for tasks to your powers, pray for power equal to your tasks. (Phillips Brooks)
- If you want to be a good person, find fault in yourself instead of finding someone's fault. (Ini Ea Mon)

- Nations do not mistrust each other because they are armed; they are armed because they do not trust each other. (Ronald Reagan)
- Only those who dare to fail greatly can ever achieve greatly. (Robert F. Kennedy)
- Life is not about getting and having; it is about growing and being. (Kevin Kruse)
- I am not a product of my circumstances; I am a product of my decisions. (Stephen Covey)
- The more you say, the less people remember. (Francois Fenelon)
- The two most important days in your life are the day you were born and the day you find out why. (Mark Twain)
- Man do not shape destiny; Destiny produces the man for the hour. (Fidel Castro)
- Whatever the mind of man can conceive and believe, it can achieve. (Napoleon Hill)
- Life is about making an impact; not making an income. (Kevin Kruse)
- It is not the oath that makes us believe the man, but the man the oath. (Aeschylus)
- Happiness is a choice that requires effort. (Aeschylus)
- It is in the character of very few men to honor without envy a friend who has prospered. (Aeschylus)

- There is no pain so great as memory of joy in present grief. (Aeschylus)
- Wisdom comes along through suffering. (Aeschylus)
- Time as we grow old teaches all things. (Aeschylus)
- Memory is the mother of all wisdom. (Aeschylus)
- I know how men in exile feed on dreams of hope. (Aeschylus)
- Tell no man happy till he is dead. (Aeschylus)
- Knowing your own darkness is the best method for dealing with the darkness of other people. (Carl Jung)
- Who looks outside, dreams; who looks inside, awakes. (Carl Jung)
- The privilege of a lifetime is to become who you truly are. (Carl Jung)
- A flower falls even though we love it; weed grows even though we do not love it. (Zen quotation)
- If you are not afraid of dying, there is nothing you cannot achieve it. (Zen quotation)
- Give a man a fish and you feed him for a day. Teach him how to fish and you feed him for a lifetime. (Zen quotation)
- In the beginner's mind there are many possibilities but in the expert's mind there are few. (Zen quotation)
- You cannot find the truth right where you are, you else do expect to find it. (Zen quotation)

- The quieter you become, the more you can hear. (Zen quotation)
- When you seek it, you cannot find it. (Zen quotation)
- Sadness flies on the wings of time. (Jean De La Fontaine)
- You are one decision away from a totally different life. (Mark Batterson)
- Everyone thinks of changing the world, but no one thinks of changing himself. (Leo Tolstoy)
- Nothing is more beautiful than a smile that has struggled through tears. (Demi Lovato)
- Whenever you find yourself on the side of the majority it is time to pause and reflect. (Mark Twain)
- The fool doesn't think he is wise but the wise man knows himself to be a fool. (Willian Shakespeare)
- Tears may be dried up but the heart may never. (Marguerite Gardiner)
- Why waste your tears on someone who makes you cry? (Kristen Dunst)
- Happiness is not a station you arrive at, but a manner of travelling. (Margaret B. Runback)
- Sometimes the questions are complicated and the answers are simple. (Dr. Seuss)
- Forgiveness does not change the past, but it does enlarge the future. (Paul Boese)

- A donkey carrying a pile of holy books is still a donkey. (Zen quotation)
- Tears are the silent language of grief. (Voltaire)
- To ask the right question is already half the satisfaction of a problem. (Carl Jung)
- If a man knows more than others, he becomes lonely. (Carl Jung)
- Good, better, best, never let it rest, till your good is better and your better is best. (St. Jerome)
- I believe if you keep your faith, you keep your trust, you keep the right attitude, if you are grateful, you will see God open up new doors. (Joel Osteen)
- You are what you do not; what you say you'll do. (Carl Jung)
- You believe God looks at us from above, but he actually sees us from the inside. (Shams Tabriz)
- Truth's place is in the heart. (Yunus Emre)
- Thanking is difficult, that's why most people judge. (Carl Jung)
- Management is doing things right, leadership is doing right things. (Peter F. Drucker)
- You can't replace loyalty, and you can't buy loyalty. (Jeff Wobig)
- Indeed, he does not like the proud. (Surah An-Nahl 16:23)

- In anger we should refrain both from speech and action. (Pythagoras)
- The true value of a leader is not measured by the work they do; a leader's true value is measured by the work they inspire others to do. (Simon Sinek)
- Bosses push, leaders pull, real leadership is servant leadership. (Dave Ramsey)
- The boss inspires fear; the leader inspires enthusiasm. (John C. Maxwell)
- What you do has far greater impact than what you say. (Stephen R. Covey)
- The function of leadership is to produce more leaders, not more followers. (Ralph Nader)
- Dear God, I just want to say "THANK YOU" for everything you have done for me. (Ameen)
- If you cannot do great things, do small things in a great way. (Napoleon Hill)
- We can't continue during the same things and expect different results. (Paulo Coelho)
- Mind is like an umbrella. It only works when it is open. (Sir James Jeans)
- None of you truly believes until he wishes for his brother what he wishes for himself. (Bukhari)
- Two things prevent us from happiness: Living in the past and observing others. (Paulo Coelho)

- The worst disease in the world is corruption, and there is a cure: transparency. (Paul David Hewson)
- Love yourself just as you are (James Bettie)
- Happiness is only real when shared. (John Ker Kauer)
- We show the children the way by our actions, so let's all wake up and show them a new way. (Tracey Smith)
- The smarter you get, the less you speak; love is a seed, if you care, it grows. (Ran Lavinia)
- The enemy isn't fighting you because you are weak. He is fighting you because you are strong. (Lance Wallnau)
- The less you respond to rude, critical, argumentative people the more peaceful your life will become. (Mandy Hale)
- Humanity is the biggest religion. (Mohammed Waris)
- There is no load as heavy as envy.... Don't carry it! (Ejiro Romar Adigbo)
- Family is not an important thing. It is everything. (Michael J. Fox)
- I have the audacity of equality. (Hasan Minhaj)
- The Prophet (SAW) said: "If the prayer is started do not run for it but just walk for it calmly and pray whatever you get and complete whatever is missed." (Sahih Al Bukhari 908)
- Patience is beautiful. (Surah Yusuf V.18)
- Kindness and love is what the world needs right now. (Tracy Smith)

- Don't be proud of your salary. Be proud of your investments. (Warren Buffett)

- If you keep breaking other people's hearts, whatever duty you perform is of no use. (Shams Tabriz)

- If you cannot be a pencil to write someone's happiness then try to be a nice eraser to remove their sadness. (Priyanjali Singh)

- When misunderstandings grow cut your ego. (Dr. Zakir Naik)

- The only person you should try to be better than, is the person you were yesterday. (Matty Muccins)

- Control your anger and ego. (Payel Koley)

- Too much ego will kill your talent. (Vicky Tambakhe)

- Live like an atom; think like the sun. (Jasper)

- The problem with introspection is that it has no end. (Philip K. Dick)

- The question is not only what have I achieved. The question is how have I helped others to achieve? That is the notion of social conscience in Islam. (The Aga Khan, Maputo)

- If you feel pain, you're alive; if you feel other people's pain, you're a human being. (Leo Tolstoy)

- Understanding is deeper than knowledge; there are many people who know you, but very few who understand you. (Robert Mugabe)

- Those who judge will never understand and those who understand will never judge. (Wilson Kanadi)
- Moon never begs for attention. (Shristy Sinha)
- There is no higher religion than human service. To work for the common good is the greatest deed. (Woodrow Wilson)
- We don't have to be smarter than the rest; we have to be more disciplined than the rest. (Warren Buffet)
- If something is wrong, fix it if you can, but train yourself not to worry; worry never fixes anything. (Ernest Hemingway)
- You don't always need to understand your journey in life, you just need to trust that you are going in the right direction. (Steven Aitchison)
- The best of deeds is the observance of power at its proper time and kindness to parent. (Misaim)
- Nobody dresses better to an event than a lady who knows her ex-husband is going to be there. (Robert Mugabe)
- Leadership is not about titles, positions or flow charts, it is about one life influencing another. (John C. Maxwell)
- The key to a successful leadership is influence; not authority. (Ken Blanchard)
- Not all readers are leaders but all leaders are readers. (Henry S. Truman)

- When the leaders lack confidence, the followers lack commitment. (John C. Maxwell)
- The successful person finds the right place for himself, but a successful leader finds the right place for others. (John C. Maxwell)
- Leadership is an action, not a position. (Donald McCannon)
- Leaders think and talk about the solution. Followers think and talk about the problems. (Brian Tracy)
- Effective leadership is not about making speeches or being liked; leadership is defined by results, not attributes. (Peter Drucker)
- People buy into the leader before they buy into the vision. (John C. Maxwell)
- A cowardly leader is the most dangerous of man. (Stephen King)
- To common is to serve, nothing more nothing less. (Andre Malraux)
- A ruler should be slow to punish and swift to reward. (Ovid)
- Sufi holy man was asked what forgiveness is; he said it is the fragrance that flowers give when they are crushed. (Sufi)
- Life asked death "why do people love me and hate you?" Death replied "because you are a beautiful lie and I'm a painful truth." (Sufi)
- Whenever a man is alone with a woman the devil makes a third. (Al- Tirmidhi 3118)

- Be honest, be humble and always listen more than you talk. (James Hilton)
- It is a terrible offence to have suspicion about someone. (Dada Bhagwan)
- You do not attract what you want, you attract what you are. (Dr. Wayne Dyer)
- Your life does not get better by chance. It gets better by change. (Jim Rohn)
- Crazy minds discuss ideas. Average minds discuss events. Lazy minds discuss people. (Eleanor Roosevelt)
- True friends are those rare people who come to find you in dark places and lead you back to the light. (Steven Aitchison)
- Have patience; all things are difficult before they become easy. (Saadi)
- If war can be started with lies, then peace can be started with truth. (Julian Assange)
- Life doesn't require that we be the best, only that we try our best. (H. Jackson Brown, Jr.)
- Nobody can go back and start a new beginning, but anyone can start today and make a new ending. (Maria Robinson)
- Action is the fundamental key to all success. (Pablo Picasso)
- You can never cross the ocean unless never have the courage to lose sight of the shore. (Christopher Columbus)

- If you don't design your own life plan, chances are you'll for into someone else planed for you. Not much. (Jim Rohn)
- Not to know certain things is a great part of wisdom. (Hugo Grotius)
- Laughing faces do not mean that there is absence of sorrow! But it means that they have the ability to deal with it. (William Shakespeare)
- As long as there are prisons, police, armies, navies, we are not civilized when the earth joins together and uses the earth intelligently; that will be the beginning of civilization. (Will Smith)
- When you are in light everything follows you, but when you enter into the dark even your own shadow doesn't follow you. (Hitler)
- Opportunities are like sunrises, if you wait too long you can miss them. (William Arthur)
- My pain may be the reason for somebody's laugh. But my laugh must never be the reason for somebody's pain. (Charlie Chaplin)
- Do not fear to be eccentric in opinion for every opinion now accepted was once eccentric. (B. Russell)
- Judge a man by his questions rather than by his answers. (Voltaire)
- Talent hits a target no one else can hit, genius hits a target no one else can see. (Arthur Schopenhauer)

- Right action is better than knowledge but to do what is right, we must know what right is. (Charlemagne)

- Breaking hearts doesn't solve problems. (Hayme Ana)

- The heaviest thing in this world is a child's dead body on a dad's shoulder. (Aditiya Shukla)

- Those who judge will never understand and those who understand will never judge. (Wilson Kanadi)

- Patience is not about the ability to wait, but the ability to keep a good attitude while waiting. (Joyce Meyer)

- I got my start by giving myself a start. (Madam C. J. Walker)

- If I have accomplished anything in life it is because I have been willing to work hard. (Madam C. J. Walker)

- It is pretty hard for the Lord to guide you if you have not made up your mind which way to go. (Madam C. J. Walker)

- America doesn't respect anything but money, what our people need is a few millionaires. (Madam C. J. Walker)

- I am not ashamed of my past; I am not ashamed of my humble beginning. (Madam C. J. Walker)

- The real tragedy of the poor is the poverty of their aspiration. (Adam Smith)

- Where there is great property there is great inequality for one very man there must be at least five hundred poor. (Adam Smith)

- Defense is superior to opulence. (Adam Smith)

- No society can surely be flourishing and happy of which for greater part of the members are poor and miserable. (Adam Smith)

- Never play with the feelings of others because you may win the game but the risk is that you will surely lose the person for a lifetime. (Shakespeare)

- Alone, I can 'say' but together we can 'talk'.
  Alone, I can 'enjoy' but together we can 'celebrate'.
  Alone, I can 'smile' but together we can 'laugh'. (Prof. Lee Tzu Pheng)

- Gratitude helps us to see what is there instead of what is not (Annette Bridges)

- It has been said that man can create anything he can imagine. (Napoleon Hill)

- A smile is a curve that sets everything straight. (Phillis Diller)

- Being honest may not get you a lot of friends but it will always get you the right ones. (John Lennon)

- I myself am Heaven and Hell. (Omar Khayyam)

- A hair divides what is false and true. (Omar Khayyam)

- Strange… is it not? That of the myriads who before us passed the door of darkness through, no one returns to tell us of the road which to discover; we must travel too. (Omar Khayyam)

- Never stop doing your best just because someone doesn't give you credit. (Kylee Clark)

- Love is when the other person's happiness is more important than your own. (M. Jackson Brown)
- Don't be afraid of losing people. Be afraid of losing yourself by trying to please everyone. Don't change your thoughts to please someone. (Ridzz)
- A finger that wipe away your tears during hard times is greater than the thousand hands that clapped for your success. (Nicks Insporoxy Goote)
- If you announce your goals to others you're less likely to succeed. Studies confirm you lose motivation. You are yours before you are anyone else's. (Ridzz)
- People can't use you, if you are useless. (Mr. Bean)
- Don't listen what people say behind you, a lion never looks back when small dogs bark. (Rebelle)
- On spending of your lazy things you do not need, soon you will have to sell things you need. (Warren Buffet)
- No matter how many you have in the end of the day, you will be alone with your problems and pain. (Gvotes Snotes)
- The secret to getting ahead is getting started. (Mark Twain)
- The calculations of confidence is better than the calculation of money. (James Madison)
- Knowledge forever governs ignorance. (James Madison)
- Liberty may be endangered by the abuse of liberty, but also the abuse of power. (James Madison)

- War should only be declared by the authority of the people whose toils and treasure are to support the burden, instead of the government which is to reap its fruits. (James Madison)
- Friends show their love in times of trouble not in happiness. (Euripides)
- Our greatest weakness lies in giving up. The most certain way to succeed is always to try just one more time. (Thomas Edison)
- Men are proven to succeed not to fail.
  (Henry David Thoureau)
- Every man needs two women. A quiet homemaker, and a thrilling nymph. (Iris Muesoch)
- The greatest deception men suffer is from their own opinions. (Leonardo Da Vinci)
- Men are like steel; when they lose their temper, they lose their worth. (Chuck Norris)
- Leadership is hard to define and good leadership even harder but if you can get people to follow you to the ends of the earth, you are a great leader. (Imsra Nooyl)
- I say to you quite frankly that the time for racial discrimination is over. (Jimmy Carter)
- We must adjust to changing times and still hold to unchanging principles. (Jimmy Carter)
- Testing oneself is best when done alone. (Jimmy Carter)

- The naked truth is always better than the best dressed lie. (Ann Landers)
- If you tell the truth, you don't have to remember anything. (Mark Twain)
- To tell the truth and make someone cry, is better than to tell a lie and make someone smile. You never find yourself until you face the truth. (Pearl Bailey)
- The world is divided into men who have wit and no religion and men who have religion and no wit. (Avicenna)
- Problems are not stop signs, they are guide lines. (Robert H. Schuler)
- There are no regrets, just lessons. (Jennifer Aniston)
- Every word has consequences, every silence too. (Jean Paul Sartre)
- Like everyone; trust no one. (Lauren Cohrad)
- It's far better to be unhappy alone than unhappy with someone. (Marilyn Monroe)
- I don't want to be alone; I want to be left alone. (Andrey Hepars)
- Being alone has nothing to do with how many people are around you. (Rkmads Yates)
- Two people can sleep in the same bed and still be alone when they close their eyes. (Haruki Murakami)
- All empires are created of blood and fire. (Pablo Escobar)

- You may be right but it doesn't mean I am wrong. (Brijesh Dalmia)
- There is no death; only a change of world. (Nature Chief Seattle)
- One day we will realize that big hearts will bring us more peace than big weapons. (A.D. Williams)
- Tears come from the heart and not from the brain. (Leonardo Da Vinci)
- Love is life, and if you miss love you miss life. (Leo Buscaglia)
- I have a thousand reasons to die and many million of tears to cry. (Draconium)
- Don't cry over someone who wouldn't cry over you. (Lauren Conrad)
- Yesterday is not ours to recover, but tomorrow is ours to win or lose. (Lyndon Johnson)
- Kill the part of you that believes it can't survive without someone else. (Sade Andriazabala)
- Life is a dream for the wise, a game for the fool, a comedy for the rich, a tragedy for the poor. (Shalom Aleicmen)
- Worry pretends to be necessary but serves no useful purpose. (Eckhart Tolle)
- What people believe prevails over the truth. (Sophocles)

- If you love two people at the same time choose the second, because if you loved the first one, you wouldn't have fallen for the second. (Johnny Depp)
- Making money is art and working is art and good business is the best art. (Andy Warhol)
- I think it would be terrific if everybody was alike. (Andy Warhol)
- Laugh as much as you breathe and love as long as you live. (Johnny Depp)
- The way to get started is to quit talking and begin doing. (Walt Disney)
- Fight for your dreams and your dreams will fight for you. (Paulo Coelho)
- Sometimes it's best to stay quiet; the silence can speak volumes without ever saying a word. (Deepak Chopra)
- Lying is done with words and also with silence. (A. Rich)
- The greatest mystery of existence, is existence itself. (Deepak Chopra)
- Only in the darkness, you are able to see the stars. (Martin Luther King)
- The most important thing is to enjoy your life, to be happy. It's all that matters. (Audrey Hepburn)
- We have to really educate ourselves in a way about who we are, what real identity is. (Deepak Chopra)

- I haven't failed. I have just found 10000 ways that didn't work. (Thomas Edison)
- Life is either a journey adventure or nothing. (Helen Keller)
- Success is simple, do what is right the right way at the right time. (Arnold H. Glashow)
- Whether you think you can or think you cannot, you are right. (Henry Ford)
- You can only be jealous of someone who has something you think you ought to have yourself. (Margaret Atwood)
- Spiteful words can hurt your feelings but silence breaks your heart. (C. S. Lewis)
- The biggest fight waged against you is by hurting your ego; not your body. (Prabakaran Thirwmalai)
- The best revenge is massive success. (Frank Sinatra)
- Our attitude towards others determines their attitude towards us. (Earl Nightingale)
- The only difference between a good day and a bad day is your attitude. (Duds S. Brown)
- You can be a moon and still be jealous of the stars. (Gary Allen)
- A competent and self-confident person is incapable of jealous in anything. (Robert A. Heimien)
- Jealousy is a lack of respect for the person you love. (Ivan Alekseyevich)

- Loving yourself isn't vanity; it is sanity. (Andre Gide)
- Do not try to impress people; always be yourself! (Bella Thom)
- Beauty is power; a smile is its sword. (John Ray)
- You must be the best judge of your own happiness. (Jane Austin)
- If you don't like what is being said, change the conversation. (Don Draper)
- Life is better when you smiling. (Karen McNair Gibbs)
- Count your age by friends; not years. Count your life by smiles; not tears. (John Lennon)
- There will always be suffering, but we must not suffer over the suffering. (Alan Watts)
- Every day may not be good but there's something good every day. (Jeanette Ehull)
- None but ourselves can free our minds. (Bob Marley)
- If you don't stand for something you will fall for anything. (Jeanette Ehull)
- You only live once but if you do it right once is enough. (Jeanette Ehull)
- Live as if you were to die tomorrow, learn as if you were to live forever. (Jeanette Ehull)
- Death ends a life, not a relationship. (Mitch Albom)

- The only place where success comes before work is in the dictionary. (Vidal Sassoon)
- Only I can change my life. No one can do it for me. (Carol Burnett)
- Know or listen to those who know. (Balthasar Gracian)
- I am not afraid. I was burnt to do this. (Jean of Arc)
- The harder the conflict, the more glorious the triumph. (Thomas Paine)
- NEVER, NEVER, NEVER give up. (Winston Churchill)
- Don't fight the problem, decide it. (George C. Marshall)
- After a storm comes a calm. (Matthew Henry)
- Things do not happen; things are made to happen. (John F. Kennedy)
- Set your goals high, and don't stop till you get there. (Bo Jackson)
- Without hard work, nothing grows but weeds. (Goson B. Hinckley)
- Be kind whenever possible, it is always possible. (Dalai Lama)
- You are never too old to set another goal or to dream a new dream. (C. S. Lewis)
- The secret of getting ahead is getting started. (Mark Twain)
- Either I will find a way or I will make one. (Philip Sidney)
- Do something wonderful, people may imitate it. (Albert Schweitzer)

- If you are going through hell keep going. (Winston Churchill)
- By failing to prepare, you are preparing to fail. (Benjamin Franklin)
- Expect problems and eat them for breakfast. (A. Montapert)
- Keep your eyes on the stars and your feet on the ground. (Theodore Roosevelt)
- Don't watch the clock; do what it does. (Sam Levenson)
- If you can dream it, you can do it. (Walt Disney)
- Start where you are, use what you have, do what you can. (Arthur Ashe)
- The most effective way to do it, it is to do it. (Amelia Earhart)
- Well done is better than well said. (Benjamin Franklin)
- Life isn't about finding yourself. Life is about creating yourself. (George Bernard Shaw)
- Once you choose hope, anything is possible. (Cristopher Reeve)
- The problem with Africa is that if they say nobody should go out, everybody will go out to see if nobody has gone out. (Robert Mugabe)
- If you don't fight for what you want, don't cry for what you lost. (Shikha Rajore)
- Lucky are those who find a true loyal friend in this fake world. (Shanti-Gurung)

- A strong friendship doesn't need daily conversation, doesn't always need to gatherers, as long as the relationship lives in the heart, true friends will never part. (Roman Raees)
- Beauty attracts the eye but personality captures the heart. (Surinder Rajput)
- If a man loves a woman's soul, he'll end up loving one woman, but if he just loves a woman's body or face, all the women in the world won't satisfy him. (Sanju Kumar)
- Everything is valuable only in two situations. First, before getting it. Second, after losing it. In between we don't realize the value of anything. (www.tamilpositioner.com)
- The only thing worse than being blind is having sight and no vision. (Cheleri Keller)
- We may encounter many defeats but we must not be defeats. (Maya Angelou)
- Don't judge each day by the harvest you reap but the seeds that you plant. (Robert Louis Stevenson)
- The only thing necessary for the triumph of evil is for a good man to do nothing. (Eamens)
- Extreme poverty anywhere is a threat to human security everywhere. (Kofi Annan)
- The best of all medicines is resting and fasting. (Benjamin Franklin)
- You can change friends but not neighbors. (Atal Bihari Vajpayee)

- Do the right thing, even when no one is looking. It's called integrity. (C. S. Lewis)
- Anger doesn't solve anything, but it can destroy everything. (Thomas S. Monson)
- The life in front of you is far more important than the life behind you. (Joel Osteen)
- The Prophet saw said: The most complete of the believers in faith is the one with the best character among them and the best of you are those who are best to your woman. (Jami AT-Tirmidhi)
- Charity Saad Bin Ubadah said: I said, oh messenger of Allah, what charity is best? He said: giving water to drink. (Sunnah Ibn Majah 36: 84)
- It's fun to have a partner who understands your life and lets you be you. (Kim Kardashian)
- You never know what the future holds or where my life will take me. (Kim Kardashian)
- A room without books is like a body without a soul. (Marcus Tullius Cicero)
- Classic … a book which people praise and don't read. (Mark Twain)
- The book that the world calls immoral are books that show the world its own shame. (Oscar Wilde)
- There are worse enemies than burning books. One of them is not reading them. (Joseph Brodsky)

- Think before you speak. Read before you think. (Fran Lebowitze)
- Books are the mirrors of the soul. (Virginia Woolf)
- All animals are equal, but some animals are more equal than others. (George Orwell)
- And when you want something, all the universe conspires in helping you to achieve it. (Paulo Coelho)
- Even the darkest night will end and the sun will rise. (Victor Hugo)
- Every man desires to live long but no man wished to be old. (Jonathan Swift)
- Get busy living or get busy dying. (Andy Dufresne)
- It is no use going back to yesterday because I was a different person then. (Lewis Carroll)
- Procrastination is the thief of time, collar him. (Charles Dickens)
- There is only one sin, and that is theft; when you tell a lie, you steal someone's right to the truth. (Khaled Hosseini)
- We can know only that we know nothing and that is the highest degree of human wisdom. (Leo Tolstoy)
- A person who won't read, has no advantage over one who cannot read. (Mark Twain)
- The book you don't read won't help. (Jim Rohn)
- One who cares is one who listens. (J. Richard Clark)

- There are many little ways to enlarge your child's world; love of books is the best of all. (Jaqueline Kennedy)
- Whenever you read a good book somewhere in the world a door opens to allow in more light. (Vera Na)
- One of the greatest gifts adults can give to their offspring and to their society is to read to children. (Carl Sagan)
- People generally quarrel because they cannot argue. (Gilbert K. Chesterton)
- The history of the world is the world's court of justice. (Friedrich von Schiller)
- The whole purpose of education is to turn mirrors into windows. (Sydney J. Harris)
- Violence is the last refuge of the incompetent. (Isaac Asimov)
- A book is a gift you can open again and again. (Garrison Keillor)
- Gambling is a sure way of getting nothing from something. (Wilson Mizner)
- How people treat you is their karma. How you react is yours. (Wayne Dyer)
- If you can't convince me, confuse me. (Harry S. Truman)
- Life is the first gift, love is the second and understanding is the third. (Marge Piercy)
- Children find everything in nothing. Men find nothing in everything. (Giacomo Leopard)

- The bad news is time flies; the good news is you are the pilot. (Michael Arhuler)
- Idleness is the key of beggary. (Charles Huddon Spurgeon)
- What children hear at home soon flies abroad. (Thomas Fuller)
- Elegance in not about being noticed; it's about being remembered. (Giorgio Armani)
- No society can surely be flourishing and happy, of which the far greater part of the members are poor and miserable. (Adam Smith)
- Our lives are like books and each day is a page; we can't erase what has already been written but we can make the next page better. (A.P.J.)
- The time is always right to do what is right. (Martin Luther King, Jr.)
- Who seeks shall find. (Sophocles)
- Know or listen to those who know. (Baltasar Gracian)
- Once you choose hope, anything is possible. (Cristopher Reeve)
- Sports is like a war without the killing. (Red Turner)
- It is better to give than receive; especially advice. (Mark Twain)
- Solitude is independence. (Hermann Hesse)

- Communication is the real work of leadership. (Nitin Mohria)
- We work to become, not to acquire. (Elbert Hubbard)
- Keep your fear to yourself but share your courage with others. (Robert Lewis Stevenson)
- Your talent is God's gift to you; what you do with it is your gift back to God. (Leo Buscaglia)
- An obedient wife commands her husband. (Benjamin Disraeli)
- I find nothing more depressing than optimism. (Paul Fussel)
- Sin is not so sinful as hypocrisy. (Francoise)
- Where there is moment there is improvement. (Rick Heiders)
- The only disability in life is a bad attitude. (Scott Hamilton)
- Those whom God wishes to destroy, he first makes them angry. (Euripides)
- Sport does not build character, it reveals it. (John Wooden)
- History is philosophy taught by examples. (Thucydides)
- When you are grateful fear disappears and abundance appears. (Anthony Robbins)
- A generation which ignores history has no past and no future. (Robert Heinen)
- Each man is the architect of his own fate. (Appius Claudius)
- Those who cannot learn from history are doomed to repeat

it. (George Santayana)

- You will never win if you never begin. (Helen Rowland)
- Awareness is empowering. (Rita Wilson)
- What we are is God's gift to us. What we become is God's gift to God. (Eleanor Powell)
- The gambler is a moral suicide. (Charles Caleb Colton)
- Giving is more a dictate of the heart than a command of the brain. (Henry A. Rosso)
- One law for the lion and the ox is oppression. (William Blake)
- United we stand, divided we fall. (George Pope Morris)
- There is no teaching to compare with example. (Sir Robert Baden Powell)
- It's choice not chance that determines your destiny. (Jean Midetch)
- The sweetest sound of all is praise. (Xenophon)
- Individually we are one drop, together we are an ocean. (Ryunosuke Satoro)
- Words are of course the most powerful drugs used by mankind. (Rudyard Kipling)
- The people's safety is the law of God. (James Otis)
- A desire to resist oppression is implanted in the nature of man. (Tacitus)
- Mistakes are merely steps up the ladder. (Paul J. Meyer)

- A well-aimed spear is worth three. (Ted Williamson)
- Personality is to a man what perfume is to a flower. (Charles M. Schwab)
- Sell no virtue to purchase wealth nor liberty to purchase power. (Benjamin Franklin)
- Great hypocrites are the real atheists. (Francis Bacon)
- All a man can betray is his consciousness. (Joseph Conrad)
- One father is more than a hundred school masters. (George Herbert)
- Humanity is the biggest religion. (Younus Al Gohar)
- Women are supposed to be very calm generally but women feel just as men feel. (Charlotte Bronte)
- If I loved you less, I might be able to talk it more. (Jane Austen)
- Happiness in marriage is entirely a matter of chance. (Jane Austen)
- Only dead fish go with the flow. (Andy Hurt)
- I have often regretted my speech; never my silence. (Xenocrates)
- Happiness resides not in possession and not in gold. Happiness dwells in the soul. (Democritus)
- The most difficult thing in life is to know yourself. (Thales of Miletus)
- Many people in the world would be scared if they saw in

the mirror not their faces but their character. (Jannat ul Firdous)

- Time is the most valuable thing that a man can spend. (Diogenes)
- Know how to listen and you will profit even from those who talk badly. (Plutarch)
- Without training they lack knowledge, without knowledge they lack confidence, without confidence they lack victory. (Julius Caesar)
- One original thought is worth a thousand mindless quotings. (Diogenes)
- The content of your character is your choice, day by day what you think and what you do is who you become. (Heracletus)
- We have two ears and only one tongue in order that we may hear more and speak less. (Diogenes)
- Experience is the teacher of all things. (Julius Caesar)
- We are more curious about the meaning of dreams than about things we see when awake. (Diogenes)
- I don't need a friend who changes when I change and who nods when I nod; my shadow does that much better. (Plutarch)
- There is nothing permanent except change. (Heracletus)
- What we achieve inwardly will change outer reality.(Plutarch)
- A day without laughter is a day wasted. (Charlie Chaplin)

- The world is changed by your example not by your opinion. (Paulo Coelho)

- No one has ever become poor by giving. (Anne Frank)

- My grandfather once told me that there were two kinds of people. Those who do the work and those who take the credit; he told me to try to be in the first group; there was much less competition. (Indira Gandhi)

- Anyone who does not love does not know God, for God is love. (L. John 4:8)

- They have money for war but can't feed the poor. (Tupac Shakur)

- A noble heart will refuse the happiness built on the misfortune of others. (Suri Saying)

- When people succeed, it is because of hard work; luck has nothing to do with success. (Diego Maradona)

- Understanding the misunderstanding is the best understanding. (Divyesh)

- My relationship with God is my number one focus; I know if I take care of that, he will take care of everything else. (Ameen)

- When you kneel down to God, he stands up for you. And when he stands there for you, no one can stand against you. (Ameen

Section 4

Life stories and lessons

Top ten reasons why reading is important:

It helps you have a career.

It keeps you from ignorance.

It helps your imagination grow.

It makes you go next grade.

It helps you learn new words.

It makes your grade go higher.

It relieves stress.

It creates self-esteem.

It helps you space properly.

It helps you later on in life.

Relationships

A mistake is a single page of life but a relationship is a complete book.

So don't lose a full book for a single page.

Being alone

Alone I can "say" but together we can "talk".

Alone I can "enjoy" but together we can "celebrate"

Alone I can "smile" but together we can "laugh".

Four beautiful thoughts of life.

Look back and get experience.

Look forward and see hope.

Look around and find reality.

Look within and find yourself.

Don't hurt anyone.

The most expensive liquid in the world is a tear;

It is 1% water and 99% feelings.

Think before you hurt someone.

Gift to Parents

If you are beautiful that is a gift from your parents.

If you make your life beautiful, that's a gift for your parents.

Confidence

Confidence is believing you're good.

Arrogance is believing you're better than anyone else.

Leaders need to be confident; not arrogant.

Confidence is better than perfection.

Perfection means doing the best, but confidence means knowing how to handle the worst.

Toxic Energy

When you cut off someone from your life,

they will never tell people the full story.

They will only tell them the part that makes you look bad and them innocent.

Four important words in life:

Love, Honesty, Truth, Respect.

Without these in your life you have nothing.

Who you should talk to.

Talk to someone who makes you happy but, never miss to

 talk with someone who feels happy to talk to you.

 Feel the difference.

Four things you can't get back:

The stone after it's thrown;

The word after it's said;

The occasion after it's missed;

and the time after it is gone.

Two important lessons for your life.

Do not follow the majority. Follow the right way.

Be like the moon, not always full. But always beautiful.

Always use branded items in life.

For lips, truth.

For voice, prayer.

For eyes, sympathy.

For hands, charity.

For heart, love and

for face, smile.

The two things that define you.

1. Your patience when you have nothing.

2. Your attitude when you have everything.

Never blame anyone in your life.

Good people give you happiness.

Bad people give you experience.

The worst people give you a lesson.

The best people give you memories.

The most wonderful places to be in the world:

In someone's thoughts.

In someone's prayers.

In someone's heart.

Important Guidelines in Life:

When you are alone, mind your thoughts.

When you are with friends, mind your tongue.

When you are angry, mind your temper.

When you are with a group, mind your behavior.

When you are in trouble, mind your emotions.

When God starts blessing you, mind your ego.

Life is a test.

If God answer your prayers he is increasing your faith.

If he delays, he is increasing your patience.

If he does not answer he has something better for you

Challenges

When you challenge people, you will lose one day.

When you challenge yourself, you will win every day.

When life puts you in tough situations

Don't say "Why me"?

Just say "Try me".

We don't grow when things are easy.

We grow when we face challenges.

How to talk:

Talk to your mother lovingly.

Talk to your father respectfully.

Talk to your wife truthfully.

Talk to your brother heartfully.

Talk to your sister affectionately.

Talk to your relatives empathetically.

Talk to your children enthusiastically.

Talk to your friends jovially.

Talk to officials politely.

Talk to vendors strictly.

Talk to customers honestly.

Talk to workers courteously.

Talk to politicians carefully.

22 ways to make progress:

1. Wake up early

2. Find inspiration

3. Learn skills

4. Read daily

5. Help others

6. Invest

7. Eat well

8. Net working

9. Save money; invest more

10. Use less

11. Get a mentor; be your self

12. Delegate is think big

13. Set goal track

14. Be productive

15. Plan your day

16. Build a brand

17. Smile more

18. Positive attitude

19. Fall fast

20. Spend wisely

21. Have a purpose

22. Be ambitious

Distance yourself from the people who:

1. Lie to you.

2. Disrespect you.

3. Use you.

4. Put you down.

Three pieces of advice:

Don't talk; act.

Don't say; show.

Don't promise; prove.

Traits of your Character

Ego - kill it.

Love - value it.

Smile - keep it.

Gossip - ignore it.

Success - achieve it.

Jealousy - distance it.

Knowledge - acquire it.

Confidence - trust it.

The prophet's Lifestyle:

Talk softly

Walk humbly

Breathe deeply

Sleep sufficiently

Dress properly

Interact politely

Act fearlessly

Work patiently

Think truthfully

Believe correctly

Behave decently

Plan orderly

Earn honestly

Spend intelligently

Sacrifice regularly

Serve parents happily

Respect neighbors appropriately

How to express condolences in Life

Please accept my sincerest condolences.

My thoughts are with you in your time of grief.

This is such a shock; my heart aches to hear the news.

My deepest sympathies to you and your family.

I am sorry beyond words for your loss.

Finding the right Woman

A man once asked his father:

"Father, how will I ever find the right woman?"

His father replied: "Forget about finding the right woman; be right man".

Material Things

When you pass away, they won't remember your car or house, they will remember who you were.

Be a good human.

Only three types of people tell the truth:

The drunk, the angry and the kids.

Happiness

Attention.

Affection.

Appreciation.

Just 3 things required to make someone happy.

Never forget two people in your life.

The person who loses everything just to make you win. (Your father)

The person who was with you in every pain. (Your mother)

Forget the Past

Don't waste your time looking back on what you've lost. Move on. For life is not meant to be traveled backwards.

Never see what has been done.

Only see what remains to be done.

Death

Death is real!

You will die alone,

be buried alone,

be questioned alone.

May God make that easy for us!

Only three types of people tell the truth:

The drunk, the angry and the kids.

Laughter

Always find a reason to laugh.

It may not add years to your life,

but it will surely add life to your years.

Palm Reading

Never believe the lines of your hands that predict your future.

Because people who don't have hands also have future.

Believe in yourself.

Spirit of True Love

To love without condition.

To talk without intention.

To give without reason.

To care without expectation.

That's the spirit of you true love.

True Friends

Good friends care for each other.

Close friends understand each other.

But true friends

Stay forever, beyond words,

Beyond distance and beyond time.

Expectations

Someone asked me, "Who hurt you"?

I replied. "My own expectations".

Comparison

Don't compare your life to others.

There's no comparison between the sun and the moon. They shine when it's their time.

Motivation

No matter how you feel:

Get up, dress up, show up and never give up.

Integrity

When you are no longer friends with someone, respect the secrets they shared with you.

It is called integrity.

Responsibility

It's not the age that make you mature.

It is the RESPONSIBILITY.

Old Flame

Never go back to an old love

no matter how strong it is.

It's like reading a book over and over again, when you
already know how it ends.

Meaning of Life

Once a wise man was asked. "What is the meaning of life?"

He replied, "Life itself has no meaning. Life is an opportunity to create a meaning."

Today's reality:

People don't make time for you when you are alone.

They make time for you when they are alone.

Trust

Try to understand people before trusting them. Because you are living in such a world where artificial lemon flavor is for welcome drinks and real lemon is used in finger bowls.

Time

It takes a minute to like someone;

An hour to love someone;

But to forget someone takes a lifetime.

Too Much

Don't trust too much.

Don't love too much.

Don't hope too much.

Because that "too much"

Can hurt you so much.

Teachings of a River

Rivers never go reverse.

So try to live like a river.

Forget your past and focus on your future.

Always be positive.

God says:

"Remember these four things:

1. I will make a way for you.

2. I'm fighting a way for you.

3. Prayer is the best medicine.

4. Trust my timing."

Two principles for a happy life

1. Use things. Not people.

2. Love people. Not things.

Characters of your Parents

No man can protect you like your father.

No woman can love you like your mother.

Words

The most selfish one-letter word "I"; avoid it.

The most satisfying two-letter word "we"; use it.

The most poisons three-letter word "ego"; overcome it.

The most loving four-letter word "love"; value it.

The most pleasing five-letter word "smile"; keep it.

The fastest spreading six-letter word "rumors"; ignore it

The hardest working seven-letter words "success"; achieve it.

The most enviable eight-letter word "jealousy"; distance it.

The most powerful nine-letter word "knowledge"; acquire it.

The most valued ten-letter word "friendship"; maintain it.

Words are like keys;

If you choose them right they can open my heart and shut any mouth.

Philosophy of life:

A man with one watch knows what time it is.

A man with two watches is never quite sure.

Friends are more important than you realize.

Just as a candle cannot burn without fire,

men cannot live without a spiritual life.

Fear is the mind killer.

Words have the power to both destroy and heal;

When words are both true and kind, they can change the world.

Actions speak louder than words.

Find your purpose.

Look within.

Be resilient.

Even death is not to be feared by one who has lived wisely.

One that confounds good and evil is an enemy of good.

Nothing turns out to be as oppressive and unjust as a feeble government.

Slavery is a weed that grows on every soil.

Sin has many tools, but lie is the handle which fits them all.

Flattery corrupts both the receiver and the giver.

Surround yourself with those who make you laugh not cry.

Those who love you, don't hurt you,

and those who appreciate you, don't use you.

Index

Printed in Great Britain
by Amazon

81936669R00180